Praise for

52 Weeks,
52 Sweets

"*52 Weeks, 52 Sweets* is a soulful journey of food. Vedika beautifully illustrates how seasonal desserts can be through her collection of childhood favourites to desserts that will impress your family and friends."

—Nick Makrides, YouTube star of *The Scran Line*

"Vedika takes her readers through a nostalgic culinary journey through all the seasons of the year. Her recipes are rich with stories of the heritage and culture that shaped the cook that she is today. Stunning photography brings her recipes to life in a delectable and approachable way."

—Christy Denney, cookbook author and food blogger of *The Girl Who Ate Everything*

"Vedika's flavor profiles are always so exciting! She has the unique ability to combine the familiar with the exotic to get us reaching outside our comfort zones to try something new. These dessert recipes will surely become new family favorites!"

—Beth Le Manach, YouTube star of *Entertaining with Beth*

"Vedika has given bakers a book that can be savored year-round. *52 Weeks, 52 Sweets* is a collection of recipes that feel both nostalgic and inventive. Each recipe is beautifully crafted to fit the season with flavor profiles that show off her diverse background. Paired with her stunning photography, this book inspires baking unique desserts week after week."

—Kristin "Baker Bettie" Hoffman, author of *Baker Bettie's Better Baking Book*

"I already know **52 Weeks, 52 Sweets: Elegant Recipes for All Occasions** will be the first of many successful cookbooks from the talented Vedika. Her desserts have a soul, they come from the heart and delight the palate. There is a story behind every recipe and the combination of flavors brings you from India to Poland to the Netherlands on a personal and indulgent dessert journey. With gorgeous photography and beautifully written recipes, Vedika will guide you with her natural charm to bake like a champion. I myself can't wait to bake my way through this delicious collection of recipes. I will definitely start with the Apple and Cardamom Cake and keep going with the Caffeine Infusion Mocha Muffins."

—Barbara Lamperti, cookbook author and creator of Buonapappa.net

"Vedika imbues her recipes with her signature 'can do' accessibility and infectious joy in the making of the dish. She writes in a way that makes even novice bakers feel like they can accomplish these treats—as they should! She doesn't lead you astray. She also provides added foodie tips that you'll use for sweet and savory creations alike. Beyond the recipes, she sprinkles her own culturally-varied global experiences throughout the pages, giving the book life and texture."

—Katie Quinn, cookbook author, YouTuber (*QKatie*), and podcaster (*Keep It Quirky*)

"What a beautiful collection of treats. The flavour combinations are enticing, and every picture makes you want to dive in and make the recipe straight away."

—Karen Barnes, editor-in-chief of *Delicious* magazine

52 Weeks,
52 Sweets

52 Weeks, 52 Sweets

Elegant Recipes for All Occasions

VEDIKA LUTHRA

CORAL GABLES

Published by Mango Publishing, a division of Mango Media Inc.

Cover Design: Elina Diaz
Layout & Design: Elina Diaz
Photos: Vedika Luthra

For permission requests, please contact the publisher at:
Mango Publishing Group
2850 S Douglas Road, 2nd Floor
Coral Gables, FL 33134 USA
info@mango.bz

For special orders, quantity sales, course adoptions and corporate sales, please email the publisher at sales@mango.bz. For trade and wholesale sales, please contact Ingram Publisher Services at customer.service@ingramcontent.com or +1.800.509.4887.

52 Weeks, 52 Sweets: Elegant Recipes for All Occasions

Library of Congress Cataloging-in-Publication number: 2021943852
ISBN: (p) 978-1-64250-668-6 (e) 978-1-64250-669-3

BISAC category code: CKB014000, COOKING / Courses & Dishes / Cakes

Printed in the United States of America

For Mom, Dad and Neha.

The sweetest of all.

Table of Contents

Foreword

As a professional pastry chef and an overall lover of dessert, I was immediately drawn to Vedika and her style of baking from the moment I met her. I have known Vedika for many years and have watched from afar as she evolved as a baker and really honed her craft and style in the kitchen. Her passion is evident in her desserts. From the oven to the plate, Vedika has not only that special touch, but also an eye for beautiful food, as you can see in her photography.

Creating a repertoire of recipes that people can have that is seasonal means the baker can focus on what to bake for the time of year using ingredients in season and flavors of the moment, be it springtime with The Best Carrot Cake or the holidays when a Festive Pavlova is exactly what you need for your family gathering. I also loved how Vedika shared a little of her Indian culture and traditional recipes throughout the book.

Whether you are a novice baker or even more advanced, I see this book being for everyone and anyone who loves baking as much as Vedika does.

Gemma Stafford
Gemma's Bigger Bolder Baking

Introduction

On Saturday mornings, my father visits our local farmers' market in Poland for the week's freshest produce. When I was younger, I'd accompany him, eager to observe the delights on display: whether it was swan-shaped squash, farm-fresh eggs from his favorite vendor, homemade plum or tomato jams, fresh bread, or antiques that I could use for my photography, there was always something that caught my eye. I enjoyed browsing through the lively stalls, immersed in the intoxicating mix of smells and hearing snippets of conversations between vendors and customers. These trips with my father instilled in me an appreciation not only for food and its power to bring people together, but also of the country I was living in, and somehow I felt more connected to my surroundings.

It is with these memories that I present you with 52 Weeks, 52 *Sweets Elegant Recipes for All Occasions*, a book that has been in the works long before I began writing it. In some ways this book is a reflection of my own story, a collection of recipes that have grown with me over the years. I began baking when I was eight; it was a therapeutic experience for me, a way to destress after school. It continues to be a form of relaxation, from the measuring, mixing, and stirring to the folding and frosting. This passion has taken me far beyond the kitchen though; what started out as a hobby soon turned into creating cooking videos (some of which amassed forty million views), starting my food blog, *Hot Chocolate Hits*, finding a love for photography and food styling, and now, writing my first cookbook—something I had only dreamed of.

I hope that, with this book, I can share my love and passion for all things sweet with you. Each recipe has been thoughtfully included, a blend of my favorites from when I started baking, some acquired from family and friends, some that I stumbled across and have been making on repeat, some that I developed especially for this book, and a few handpicked from the blog. All delicious, all written with care. In writing this book, I wanted to convey a personal journey. For this reason, the theme of this book is both seasonal and cultural, family favorites that can be made throughout the year, each with a story. I was born in India, raised in Poland and moved to the Netherlands in pursuit of further education. My multicultural background introduced me not only to a variety of people but also to a variety of cultures and cuisines, and it is this perspective that built the backbone of this book. The Apple and Cardamom Cake (p. 135) is a fusion of my Indian roots and Polish upbringing, and the *Kersenflappen*, Cherry Hand Pies (p. 119), are inspired by my time living in the Netherlands. These recipes bring you a medley of flavors, using seasonal fruits, swirls of spices, and bold combinations.

They are not traditional *per se*, but they are authentic. And whether you are a novice in the kitchen or a more experienced baker, there is something here for everyone.

A Few Words about This Book

My aim with 52 Weeks, 52 *Sweets* is to provide you with a repertoire of inspired recipes to make throughout the year. The book is arranged according to month and season, based on yearly festivities as well as what produce is available. December, for instance, is all about the holidays, whereas January is aimed at healthier eating after the winter festivities. Although these recipes are organized chronologically, you can enjoy them year-round. So even if it isn't November, you can still savor the dark, sumptuous chocolate pie (p. 171) whenever you please, as it is sure to be a favorite at any time of the year.

Seasonal Ingredients

Not only will you be living more sustainably by using seasonal, locally sourced produce, but your finished dessert will be far tastier, because ingredients that are in season are at their ripest, and most fragrant. What's in season will depend on where exactly on the planet you find yourself. For instance, in India, mangoes are ubiquitous in late spring and summer, whereas in Poland it is berries and cherries that are prevalent during these months. Most of the recipes in this book call for seasonal fruit (and vegetables in some cases) in Europe and North America, but these recipes can very easily be adjusted to what you can source locally. If you don't have apples, try pears, or perhaps plums or strawberries. I try to list suggestions in the recipe itself, but you can get really creative here: if you feel inspired by the fresh produce you find, why not use it in one of the recipes? Usually, you know things are in season if they take up multiple consecutive sections in supermarkets or farmers' markets. In winter, a small pack of raspberries costs perhaps five times as much as during the summer when it's in season—another reason to bake seasonally.

Spices

Spices and herbs enhance the flavor of food (along with providing various nutritional benefits), so why not incorporate them in desserts? You might be pleasantly surprised by even the most unconventional combinations, whether it's adding a pinch of cayenne pepper to chocolate cupcakes, or a touch of thyme to your shortbread cookies. In this book, most recipes calling for spices are placed in the colder months of the year, because they add a certain warmth to the recipe that you won't want to miss. Ground ginger, nutmeg, and cinnamon are some of my favorites, as is cardamom. Cardamom is a popular addition in Indian meals and confections. Like cinnamon, it brings a warm, fragrant, slightly sweet flavor and a certain complexity to desserts. Of course, you can opt out of using the listed spices, but if you're looking for a way to make your dessert better and bolder, spices are the way to go.

Baking Essentials

Recipes are guides. They are designed to help you achieve the perfect result based on tested recipes. If you're a novice in the kitchen, it is key to your success to follow what the recipe says. After all, instructions are there for a reason. Baking, while rewarding, is not always forgiving. It requires accuracy and precision. Every single off-measurement or mishap can have consequences. For this reason, I've provided you with some essential information to help you read and understand each recipe. I also want to say that, although baking and dessert-making might require a certain level of precision, you may not always have to follow every single detail prescribed by a recipe. Being able to modify or adapt a recipe to your liking comes with experience and often a lot of trial and error. In this section, you'll find essential baking tips to keep in mind, more about key ingredients used in this book, and substitutions you might be able to use.

My Favorite Tools

What I always make sure to have when baking is a rubber spatula and a whisk. These utensils have helped me indulge my baking addiction through college. The whisk incorporates all the ingredients together in an efficient way, and the spatula leaves no drop behind. Of course, you can use an electric mixer to speed things up, but there's nothing you can't do with a whisk. It might take a little longer, but it gives you a good workout and makes you feel like you're actually doing something, rather than letting a machine do all the work for you. I occasionally make an exception for the electric mixer when I do meringues or frostings, although both of those can also be done by hand—just keep mixing! Finally, I like using a food processor for achieving fine textures, such as cookie crumbs or ground nuts, but using a Ziploc bag and a rolling pin for the first and a mortar and pestle for the second also does the trick, although it does require a bit more elbow grease.

Getting Started

As you flip through this book, your eye lingers on the Chocolate Stout Cake. Intrigued, you decide it will be your dessert for the evening. What do you do next? Well, I would start by reading the recipe. Make a list, get out your ingredients. Then read the recipe again before making it. This helps speed things up. I normally measure things as I go along, but if you're more organized than I am (which is probably a good thing) and don't want to miss an ingredient, you can premeasure everything. Next, preheat the oven and grease and, if called for, line your cake tin with parchment paper: this will also save time. When you finish preparing the mixture or batter, read through the ingredients again to make sure you've added everything (just the other day, I was making the chocolate chip cookies, see p. 53, and I forgot the egg. That's what happens when you think you know the recipe by heart and don't even look at the ingredient list!).

Measuring (Cups, Grams, and More)

Cups and milliliters measure volume, while grams and ounces measure weight. In much of Europe, we use the metric system (grams, liters, centimeters). In the United States, cups are used for baking, as are Imperial measurements (ounces, pounds, inches). Converting volume to mass is more challenging, which is why I've done all the work for you. I have to say that I use both measurements interchangeably since I work with recipes from all over the world. Grams do provide more accurate results, particularly with dry ingredients, since you can pack down a cup of flour and this can make a difference in the recipe. If you're new to the kitchen, I would recommend using weight measurements (except in the case of liquids, where volume works well).

How to Measure Correctly

With grams, measuring is easier, because you get consistent and precise measurements. You need a scale and have to make sure to set your scale to zero each time you use it. With cups, things get slightly more complex. You need to make sure that the cup is completely full. To do this, you can spoon your ingredient in, tablespoon by tablespoon, then drag a knife over the surface of the cup to make sure it's precisely one cup. If you are using a measuring cup that goes above the amount you are measuring, set the cup down on a flat surface and try to make sure the level of your ingredient is as even as possible. Don't tap the cup onto a surface to settle it, as that will remove the air and pack the ingredient, something you don't always want. Note that brown sugar needs to be packed into the cup, whereas packing flour into a cup will mean that you might have more flour than is necessary. For flour, it's best to sift it first and then place it in the cup or spoon it in rather than pack it. A heaping cup means a cup plus a few tablespoons, whereas a scant cup means just under a cup.

How to Properly Grease a Cake Pan

Greasing a cake pan is mostly required for baked goods or firmer desserts that you want to remove from the tin (think fudge, brownies, and bars or cakes), not for puddings and such.

The most effective way to grease a cake tin is to generously butter it, then line the bottom with parchment paper and dust the sides with flour. I like to use room-temperature butter to grease the pan. I then use a rubber brush to spread the mixture (rubber because the straw brushes tend to leave behind some of their bristles, and that's the last thing you want in your cake). Sometimes, I use a paper towel when I can't find the brush—just be careful that no paper towel is left behind in the cake tin.

Next comes the parchment paper. I usually trace the cake pan on the parchment using a pencil, then cut out the shape and stick it, pencil-side-down, to the bottom of the cake pan. The reason I like both butter and parchment is that, in addition to grease, the butter helps the parchment paper stick to the pan. You can also add a tablespoon of flour to the baking tin and shake it over the sink or over a work surface, letting the flour completely coat the sides before letting the excess fall out. This will ensure minimal sticking, but the flour isn't always necessary or desired, particularly in cakes that you don't frost. Buttering the sides may suffice.

This is what I do for layer cakes and springform tins. For loaves, I use a loaf liner (which is almost like a cupcake liner, but for loaves). For a cookie tray, you can just use a sheet of parchment paper or a silicone mat. For brownies or traybakes, you don't need to grease the entire tin—you can dot the corners with butter and place a large sheet of parchment over it. You can create a slit in each corner, so the paper doesn't bunch up at the ends. It depends on how neat you want to be with the look of your dessert. If you're serving the dessert in the dish itself, greasing it with butter (and perhaps dusting with flour) is enough; there's no need for the parchment.

Storing Desserts

Although it depends on what you make, baked goods are generally best enjoyed fresh, particularly ones containing fruit or fresh cream. Things like Almond Toffee (p.181) will last longer, as do frozen desserts such as homemade Ice Cream (p. 97). Each recipe contains a brief note at the end on what I think would be the ideal time to store it if necessary.

If you prefer to make desserts ahead of time, cakes can be frozen. Once the cake has cooled, wrap it tightly, *twice*, in plastic wrap (cling film) or press-and-seal wrap then wrap again in foil. These freeze for around three months. You can do the same with muffins. In both cases, it is best to freeze loaves, cakes, and cupcakes unfrosted, then add the frosting when you're ready to serve.

Although I try to bake and eat things fresh, one thing I do like to freeze is cookie dough. It is easiest to freeze balls of cookie dough, then, when you're ready, simply place the mounds on a parchment-lined baking sheet and add 1 to 2 extra minutes to the total baking time. You'll have fresh cookies whenever you like. Of course, you can freeze a container of cookie dough, but you'll need to let it thaw before baking, which takes more time.

Mixing

Most of my recipes have been developed using minimal equipment. As I mentioned earlier, the two main utensils I use when baking are a whisk and a spatula. Recipes can also be made using only a wooden spoon, or a stand mixer or electric beater if you have one. I use an electric beater when "creaming" ingredients, or mixing butter and sugar together until fluffy. The more you whip the two, the lighter your cake will be. The main thing is to make sure that you don't overmix batter after adding the flour, because overmixing ingredients could have the opposite result. In the case of a vanilla cake, for example, mixing the finished batter too much could overwork the gluten, resulting in a dense and tough cake.

Ovens

The standard oven temperature for baked goods is 180°C, which is equivalent to 350°F. Each recipe in this book lists the specific baking temperature in both scales. What scale you are familiar with likely depends on where in the world you find yourself. In Europe, we use Celsius; in the US, the norm is Fahrenheit. Note that these specifications are for conventional ovens. Fan (convection) ovens will require lower temperatures, so make sure that you are well acquainted with your oven.

For the most accurate baking results, it is helpful to use an oven thermometer. Sometimes, the temperature that you set your oven to might differ from what the temperature actually is, particularly in older ovens. This can have disastrous consequences for your baking. For instance, it might cause your cake to burn (even though the inside may not be cooked). Small tricks like keeping an oven thermometer will help things go smoothly, at least on the baking end.

Lastly, as tempting as it is, try to open the oven door as little as possible when baking, and for as little time as you can. Opening the oven door will cause some of the hot air to escape and will result in fluctuations of baking temperature.

Important Ingredients

Sugar

This book mainly calls for granulated sugar, or castor sugar, and brown sugar. When recipes call for granulated sugar, I often use demerara sugar, which has the same texture as granulated sugar, but contains a touch of molasses. The molasses adds a subtle caramel undertone to the sugar, making it more flavorful.

Substitutes

As always, I recommend adhering to what the recipe says. Using a combination of brown sugar and granulated sugar in cookies means you'll have a crispy and a chewy cookie. The granulated sugar helps with the crunch, and the brown sugar helps with the moisture.

If you're looking for low-sugar alternatives, you can try coconut sugar, or 1:1 sugar substitutes such as xylitol. Note that, particularly with the latter, you might end up with a different consistency and flavor. I've tried sugar substitutes successfully in brownies and banana cake, recipes that have flavorful ingredients to mask the slight bitterness that sweeteners add. I wouldn't recommend liquid sweeteners in place of sugar if you're looking to keep the texture and consistency of the dessert the same. It works in things like pancakes, but not as well in cakes.

Brown Sugar

Demerara sugar is a variety of brown sugar, but it is coarser. The brown sugar I refer to in the recipes is the packed variety, a moist sugar such as Muscovado, which has a higher molasses content. The browner the sugar, the more molasses is in it. I prefer to use dark brown sugar in cookies, but a lighter brown sugar works too: what you're looking for is a texture similar to that of damp sand.

Brown sugar can be replaced with granulated sugar and its substitutes; just note the difference in flavor and texture. In things like chocolate chip cookies, this matters more; in other recipes, like cakes or brownies, perhaps not as much. If you can't find brown sugar, you can make it at home.

Fat

Fat is an important element in cakes and the like. It adds moisture and improves the texture and structure of your baked goods.

Butter

Most of the recipes in this book call for unsalted butter, as I like to have control over the salt quantity I add. Salted butter works fine too, but make sure to omit the extra salt that the recipe calls for. It's best to use softened butter in cakes and such because it makes it easier to combine with other ingredients. This is essentially butter at room temperature. In pie crusts and toppings for some crumbles, however, cold butter is key. You don't want it to incorporate completely with the other ingredients when putting it together. This actually creates tiny air pockets while baking that make the dough nice and flaky.

Tip: Make your own butter. In the second grade, my class made our own butter by placing heavy whipping cream in a jar and taking turns shaking until it became solid—but this method does take a while. With some help from kitchen appliances, it's quite easy to make your own butter if you're up for a challenge. All you'll need is heavy whipping cream (see below). Whip the cream or run it in a blender till it separates completely. The liquid, or whey, is buttermilk that can be enjoyed by the glass or be used in baking. When the cream separates, place a cheesecloth over a bowl and strain the mixture. Lift the cheesecloth and bunch the top, encircling the butter, and squeeze to release all the liquid. Place the butter in a bowl. Use this in your recipes or add salt and herbs for a savory snack.

Softened Butter

Most recipes for cakes and cookies call for softened butter, or butter at room temperature. The consistency you're looking for is soft enough to push your finger into easily, a creamy texture. You can take your butter out of the fridge a few hours before using, but often I cheat. I'll put it in a bowl on top of the heater when it's winter, or if it's nice and hot during the summer, I leave it in a covered bowl outside. Mostly, I just put it in the microwave for a few seconds till it reaches that texture—just make sure not to melt or heat it too much (in which case you'll need to cool it down to room temperature).

Oil

Although oil doesn't help with leavening like butter does, it does add a nice moisture to baked goods. Most often I use flavorless oils, such as sunflower, vegetable, or canola oil. You can also replace in recipes calling for oil with olive oil or coconut oil, but keep in mind their extra flavor. In some recipes, I love using olive oil, which has a 100 percent fat content, as opposed to butter with 80 percent. This yields a richer dessert.

Oil versus Butter: Sometimes it is possible to substitute oil for butter or vice versa, but keep in mind the texture of the baked good might be different, as might the flavor. It really depends on the recipe at hand. Butter improves leavening, adds a nice familiar flavor, and helps with browning. Replacing it with oil in cake could yield a denser product, but not always (see my Chocolate Stout Cake on p. 69, which uses oil instead of butter and is super fluffy and moist).

I have successfully replaced butter with oil in banana cakes, bread, and chocolate cake. I've also tried using olive oil instead of butter in chocolate chip cookies (see p. 53), with a delicious result. Olive oil does have a distinct flavor, adding an earthy undertone. It works well in some recipes, such as the orange olive oil cake (p. 83), but proceed with caution, as its taste may not suit all recipes. Generally, I advise sticking to the recipe to get the best results, but if you realize you are out of butter in the midst of baking, you can always try replacing it with oil and see how it turns out, with the disclaimer that the result might be different.

Buttermilk

It often happens that, when I start baking, I realize I don't have buttermilk on hand. Buttermilk is acidic, and not only helps with leavening but also produces a light, fluffy, and moist cake.

Tip: Substituting buttermilk. You can make your own buttermilk substitute at home by adding 2 teaspoons of apple cider vinegar, plain vinegar, or lemon juice to each cup of milk you use. This works fine with non-dairy milk too, such as almond milk or soy milk. Let it sit for a few minutes, and it will clump and thicken. This works like magic in the place of buttermilk. You can also go old-school and make buttermilk from scratch—see the "Make your own butter" tip on page 21.

Milk

In some desserts, it's best to use full-fat milk—which is around 3.2 percent—such as in the *Gajar Halwa* (Indian carrot pudding, p. 159) or in the pudding for Regal Mango Trifle (p. 93), because it makes the dessert richer and creamier. Of course, you can use milk with a lower fat percentage for the recipes above, but the result may not be precisely the same. In cakes, I usually use 2 percent milk.

Chocolate

In recipes that call for chocolate, it is important to use a good-quality variety or chocolate that you enjoy eating plain, because the taste of chocolate is rather prominent. I use chocolate with at least 50 percent cacao solids, which in the US is referred to as semi-sweet chocolate, and in the UK as plain chocolate. You can also use a darker variety if you like. Some recipes, such as the Chocolate Log (p. 185), don't work quite as well if you use chocolate with a lower cacao content (like milk chocolate) as the consistency isn't quite right. As a rule of thumb, I'd say chocolate with at least 50 to 60 percent cacao solids works nicely.

Cream Cheese

Spreadable cream cheeses often have a thinner consistency than other varieties designed specifically for cooking. I use what I can source locally (so sometimes it does end up being the spreadable variety). Just know that the consistency of your cheesecake batter or your cream cheese frosting will be slightly thinner. In the Netherlands, the Mon Chou brand works well for frostings and the like, and in the US, try to find a block of cream cheese to work with as they are designed for cooking. If cream cheese isn't available, you can replace it with thick Greek-style yogurt (or hung curd), but this might alter the texture and flavor of the recipe. You can also replace it with mascarpone cheese or ricotta, or you can make your own!

> *Tip*: Make your own cream cheese. For each liter (quart) of whole milk, you'll need 2 to 3 tablespoons of fresh lemon juice. Bring the milk to a simmer, then slowly add in the lemon juice till it separates completely. After a few minutes, the milk solids will split completely. Then place a cheesecloth (or fine-mesh cloth) over a bowl and strain the mixture, leaving it there for around 10 to 15 minutes, until it cools and the water drains. Place the curds in a food processor and blend for several minutes or until smooth and creamy. It might take a few minutes, and scrape down the blender as necessary. Finish with a pinch of salt.

Confectioners' Sugar (Icing Sugar)

In Poland and in the Netherlands, confectioners' sugar or icing sugar translates to powdered sugar. I found this confusing when I first started baking in Poland, because most recipes call for "icing sugar" or "confectioners' sugar." Essentially it's the same thing: a finely ground sugar that is used to finish cakes or make frostings.

> *Tip*: Make your own confectioners' sugar. You can make your own at home by adding sugar and a touch of cornstarch to a food processor, then blending till fine. For every two cups of sugar, you'll need about a tablespoon of cornstarch. The cornstarch prevents the sugar from clumping and keeps it dry. You'll need to blitz the sugar for several minutes, as you don't want granules which will cause grittiness. Before using, it is best to sift confectioners' sugar to prevent lumping.

Cornstarch

Cornstarch is also referred to as "corn flour" in some recipes. Don't confuse it with cornmeal, or the yellowy flour ground from dried corn kernels. Cornstarch is a fine, white powder that resembles icing sugar. It is used to thicken sauces, and when paired with flour, helps soften the protein to yield a lighter crumb.

Vanilla

I add vanilla extract to almost everything I bake because it adds a sweet, aromatic scent to baked goods. Note that vanilla extract does not always mean the same thing as vanilla essence or imitation vanilla. In Poland, the latter is a clear liquid that comes in tiny bottles. It contains artificial flavor compounds, whereas vanilla extract is made from vanilla beans. You only need a drop or two of vanilla essence (trust me, I've tried it, and you don't want more than that). Vanilla extract, on the other hand, is fragrant and darker in color. Most recipes will call for 1 to 3 teaspoons.

Vanilla Sugar

You can also use vanilla sugar, or sugar infused with vanilla bean (commonly available in Europe) to flavor your desserts. Replace some of the regular granulated sugar with vanilla sugar. Use 1 to 2 sachets.

Vanilla Bean

Vanilla beans are slightly more expensive to use than vanilla extract but can be used to flavor desserts with mellower flavors, such as vanilla cakes and cream-based desserts (the no-churn ice cream and no-bake biscuit cake are examples, see p. 97 and p. 109). To use a vanilla bean, you'll need to slit the bean lengthwise and scrape out all the seeds using a sharp knife. In stovetop desserts, such as custard (p. 93), I often add the skin as well as the scraped seeds, and remove the skin once it's ready. The skin helps infuse the vanilla flavor into the custard.

Vanilla Bean Paste

Vanilla bean paste is the thicker, syrupier sister of vanilla extract, speckled with flecks of vanilla bean. It can be used interchangeably with vanilla extract, so substitute it in a 1:1 ratio when you wish to replace extract with vanilla bean paste.

Tip: Making your own vanilla extract. If you like, you can also make it at home. All you need is 4 to 6 vanilla beans, and 250 mL / 8.5 fl oz or 1 cup of vodka, bourbon, brandy, or rum. Create an incision along each vanilla bean using a sharp knife, and place in an airtight glass bottle or jar. Add the alcohol (use a funnel to make it easier), making sure the beans are fully submerged. Let it sit for at least eight weeks or, for maximum flavor, a year or longer (it takes a while, but is worth it!), giving it a shake every few weeks. Once you start using it, you can add more alcohol to continue the extraction process. If you notice the flavor diluting, you can always replace some of the beans with fresh ones. This stuff lasts for years and makes a great gift.

Leavening Agents

In a nutshell, leavening agents help your cake rise and help your cookies spread and rise just the right amount. There are several varieties of leavening agents. This book calls for baking soda, baking powder (sometimes a combination of the two), and active dry yeast. All of these have different properties and flavors, which is an important factor to keep in mind as you go about a recipe.

Baking Soda and Baking Powder

Baking soda, also known as sodium bicarbonate, is a base. It reacts with the acidic components in your batter, releasing carbon dioxide and creating the tiny bubbles in your cake that help it rise. Usually, it is accompanied by acidic ingredients, such as vinegar and buttermilk, in baking recipes (though not always). It is faster-acting than baking powder.

Baking powder, on the other hand, is more neutral. It is a milder version of baking soda, containing a small amount of baking soda in addition to a dry acid (such as cream of tartar) and cornstarch. Note that baking soda is around 3 times stronger than baking powder, so baking powder has a longer reaction time. Some recipes call for both, because they act slightly differently. I do not recommend substituting one for the other in recipes.

Both baking soda and baking powder need to be fresh in order to work. If you use old, opened sachets of either, it might affect the leavening of baked goods. You can test this by dissolving a bit of either in a small dish with some lukewarm water. If it starts to bubble, you're good to go!

Yeast

Yeast for breads exists in two main forms: fresh and dry. Fresh yeast is found in the refrigerator section and is not available everywhere (although it's quite easy to find in Poland!). Dry yeast, either in the form of instant yeast or active dry yeast, has a longer shelf life and comes in small packages, usually in the baking section of the grocery store. It is best to use dry yeast as soon as you open the package, and it should be stored at room temperature. Instant yeast usually results in more rapid rising, but both instant and active dry can be used interchangeably. Instant yeast can be mixed directly into your dry ingredients and doesn't require proofing (mixing with warm water to activate) beforehand, whereas active dry yeast does.

Proofing Yeast

Recipes usually explain how to proof yeast. This is done with fresh and active dry yeast. The process involves combining the yeast with lukewarm water or milk (and perhaps a touch of granulated sugar) so that the yeast can activate. You should do this in a relatively warm environment. It takes a few minutes for the yeast to activate: you'll know it's there when it becomes frothy. At that point you can add the mixture to the dry ingredients in the recipe.

Cocoa Powder

For some of the chocolatey recipes in this book, you'll need unsweetened cocoa powder. The latter exists in several varieties; the most common for baking are Dutch process cocoa powder and natural unsweetened cocoa powder. Dutch process cocoa powder is the variety most available in Europe and is neutral in that it does not react with acids or bases. Since it doesn't react with baking soda, it is usually accompanied by baking powder in recipes, unless there are other ingredients that can react with the baking soda to help the cake rise (think buttermilk or Guinness, see p.69). Natural unsweetened cocoa powder is more on the acidic side, and more bitter. This acidic property means that it reacts with baking soda to help a cake rise. Most recipes in this book were tested using Dutch process cocoa powder, but natural unsweetened cocoa powder will also work fine (you may end up with a slightly taller cake than if you use Dutch process cocoa).

Heavy Whipping Cream

Desserts usually call for heavy whipping cream, which contains 36 percent fat solids. Normal whipping cream can have 30 percent fat solids. It works fine too, but heavy whipping cream is richer and my preference for a beautiful topping to many desserts.

Flour

There are many different kinds of flour available, particularly when you get into the grains. This book calls for *all-purpose (or plain)* flour and whole wheat flour. For baking, self-rising flour, cake flour, and whole wheat pastry flour are popular options. The first, self-rising flour, has additional baking powder and salt. The second, cake flour, has a lower protein content (but can be made at home by mixing all-purpose flour with cornstarch, see below). The third, whole wheat flour, has a higher protein content, but whole wheat pastry flour has a lower content. I usually work with all-purpose and regular whole wheat flour. They are the most available around the world.

Substituting Flours

It is possible to substitute types of flour, but note that the texture of your baked good will change. For instance, if you want to replace all-purpose flour with self-rising flour, you can do so in recipes calling for baking powder, and then omit the added baking powder. If you want to replace the all-purpose flour with cake flour, you can do so, but might end up with a slightly different, maybe more fragile, texture. You can try other flours, such as spelt flour or buckwheat flour too, but these will alter the flavor and texture of the cake, so tread carefully. You might like to try combining protein-rich flours in small quantities with all-purpose flour for the first try, to see whether you like the taste and whether the texture is any different, and then add more the next time you make the recipe.

Gluten-Free Options

If you are gluten-intolerant, gluten-free flour blends can also be used in place of all-purpose flour. These should be available at your store and can usually be substituted in a 1:1 ratio for all-purpose flour. Of course, the texture of some cakes might be slightly different, but check the flour blend you use for specifications.

Veganizing Recipes

A vegan diet is one that excludes animal products, including eggs, dairy, and meat. Although many sweet recipes call for butter, eggs, and milk, most of the time these ingredients can be substituted. I usually recommend sticking to the recipe as written, but sometimes vegan substitutes work flawlessly; other times there are minor taste alterations. You'll just have to try it and see.

Eggs

Eggs do wonders for desserts. They help with the binding, structure, texture, and richness in baked goods and act as a thickener or emulsifier in custards. For these reasons, eggs may not always be easily replaced. However, many of my viewers don't eat eggs or prefer vegan alternatives.

For this reason, quite a few recipes in this book are egg-free, such as the Courgette Cake and the Chocolate Stout Cake, and where I can, I have listed suggestions for egg replacements.

These are tried, tested, and delicious. My blog (hotchocolatehits.com) also contains many other eggless recipes, so take a look, in case you like a recipe idea but need a good eggless base recipe. If you do come across a recipe calling for eggs in cakes, I don't necessarily advise substituting them unless you're in the mood for some experimentation, because it may not work out as you hope.

Egg Replacements

- In cookie dough (see p. 53), replace each egg with 4 tablespoons of milk. Non-dairy milk works fine too, if you're not vegan.

- For an egg wash (think pies and pastries), you can use heavy whipping cream instead of egg (if you are a vegan, you can use a cream substitute such as soy cream).

- You can try aquafaba (4 tablespoons per egg). Aquafaba is the thick, starchy water that you find in a can of chickpeas. Drain the chickpeas and save this water. You can use it as an egg replacement.

- Some stores have egg-replacement alternatives. Make sure to check the instructions on the package to see how to substitute it.

- You can try to replace each egg with 4 tablespoons of yogurt, buttermilk, or applesauce.

- Flax eggs: replace each egg with 1 tablespoon flax seed mixed with 3 tablespoons water. This works well in pancakes and the like but can make cakes denser.

- In custards (the mango trifle, for instance), I don't recommend actually replacing egg yolks, but I have tried vanilla pudding without eggs. You'll need to amp up the amount of cornstarch. It may not be quite as rich, but if you add a good amount of vanilla, the pudding will still be delicious and work beautifully in a trifle.

In my experience, substitutes can change the texture of baked goods. But you will never know unless you try, and experimentation in baking is fun!

Butter

Substitute butter with vegan butter (if available). I also like to use coconut oil: refined has a less prominent flavor, and unrefined will give you a slight coconut taste. I don't mind it, but it depends on the dessert. Olive oil and vegetable oil may also be used, but these might make the dessert slightly denser.

Chocolate

Use a dark chocolate made without dairy.

Cream Cheese

I've seen grocery stores sell vegan cream cheese—in my experience, this is probably the easiest thing to use. You can try using silken tofu; see my vegan chocolate tofu mousse for an idea (p. 35).

Sweetened Condensed Milk

You can replace sweetened condensed milk with sweetened condensed *coconut* milk (yes, this exists!). It is also possible to make your own by simmering any non-dairy milk with sugar.

> *Tip:* Make your own sweetened condensed milk. For 500 mL / 16.9 fl oz (2 cups) of non-dairy milk, you'll need 150 g / 5.3 oz (⅔ cup) granulated sugar, and you'll need to simmer it over low heat until it starts to caramelize slightly and turns a light cream color, stirring every now and then, for around 40 to 45 min.

Milk

Generally, milk can be replaced with non-dairy alternatives such as soy milk, almond milk, cashew milk, and oat milk. It depends on the recipe you make, because sometimes milk alternatives have a strong flavor. In the healthy whole wheat pancake recipe, see p. 41, using oat milk won't make much difference, but if you use oat milk to make the vanilla custard for the mango trifle, p. 93, it may not taste quite as nice. You may want to use a milder-flavor milk, like soy, instead.

Heavy Whipping Cream

I have replaced heavy whipping cream with coconut cream. You can either use a can of chilled coconut cream or refrigerate a can of full-fat coconut milk and remove the thick layer that forms on the top. This is crucial: if there is no thick layer, it won't whip. Place the chilled coconut cream (just the thick layer) in a bowl with your vanilla extract and whip accordingly, adding sugar to taste. You'll end up with a little over 300 mL / 10.1 fl oz (1¼ cups) of whipped coconut cream.

A Note on Troubleshooting

Each recipe in this book has been tested and retested several times to ensure that you end up with a creation resembling what is depicted in the photographs. Sometimes, though, things happen, and it might not quite work out the way you were envisioning. Why? Well, if you recall science from grade school, it is possible that your independent, dependent, and controlled variables might be slightly off. It really depends on the recipe before you. Sometimes humidity or altitude cause slightly different results. Other times your leavening agents may not have been fresh. If you substituted ingredients such as eggs, that could have been the pitfall. Did you use the right ingredients, and did you measure correctly? Did you overmix the batter? Did you add the ingredients in the right sequence? Was your oven temperature correct? Did you use an oven thermometer? Did you open the oven door while your cake was baking? Did you wait long enough? Did you use parchment paper to line your cookie tray? As you can see, there are countless possibilities for what could have gone wrong. Baking, like anything, takes practice.

I want this book to be as accessible as possible to all my readers. Of course, sometimes issues do arise. To understand what went wrong, it's helpful to reread the recipe and see where you could have made errors. And if you're really stuck, you're probably not the only one. You can always reach out to me via the blog, and I'll do my best to help you.

How to Read the Recipes

Each recipe contains a brief description, the oven temperature, the **preparation time** (time spent preparing the batter and ingredients), the **total cooking time** (for instance, the baking duration or cooking duration combined), and the number of **servings** the recipe makes.

Additionally, recipes with an asterisk (*) have notes beneath the recipe that contain helpful pointers. I would suggest reading each recipe carefully before starting it to make sure you have an idea of what you need to do. It's also helpful to measure out everything in advance to make sure you have what you need and that you're not forgetting anything.

Abbreviations:
g = grams
oz = ounces
fl oz = fluid ounces
tsp = teaspoons
tbsp = tablespoons
(*) = notes

And without further ado, let's begin!

January

January marks the first month of a new year, and brings with it new goals, resolutions, and beginnings. Healthy eating is often a part of that, so these recipes have been chosen with good health in mind.

January also brings with it frigid temperatures (at least in the Northern Hemisphere, where I live), and short days. Comfort food therefore becomes a necessity. With these two ideas in mind, I am sharing easy, healthy, yet comforting dessert recipes for January, that don't compromise one bit on taste. These recipes will help you keep your resolutions and are sure to become year-round favorites, starting with a Magical Chocolate Mousse, a healthier take on a classic dessert. Next are the No-Bake Brownies, a popular recipe with my YouTube viewers, followed by the Chia Seed Pudding, a recipe I make for breakfast and for dessert. It is packed with nutrition and will satisfy sugar cravings. Another breakfast favorite is my Fluffy Banana and Oat Pancake recipe, a hearty and satisfying treat to kickstart the day. The Peanut Butter and Date Energy Bites recipe is a sweet pick-me-up when you're on the go. Finally, my Morning Glory Muffins are a great breakfast for the whole family! With this selection of (pretty) healthy, warming recipes, you will be ready to conquer the new year.

Magical Chocolate Mousse

Prep time: 5 min

Cook time: 2–5 min

Makes: 4–6 servings

Ingredients

170 g / 6 oz (1 cup) chocolate of your choice (I like dark, but milk, or both is fine too!)

340 g / 12 oz (or 1 block) silken tofu at room temperature

60 mL / 2 fl oz (¼ cup) milk, warmed*

2 tablespoons maple syrup (or any sweetener you like, such as agave syrup)

¼ teaspoon instant espresso powder (optional)

A handful of raspberries (optional)

To garnish: raspberries; shelled, roughly chopped pistachios; chocolate curls (optional)

After you look at the ingredient list for this recipe, you'll probably think, "How on earth does this work?" but I promise you, it does. I'm not a fan of using unconventional ingredients in baking, even in the name of health, but on this one I have to acquiesce. Somehow (don't ask me how) a block of tofu transforms into a silky chocolate pudding—and unless you're the *chef de cuisine*, you'd never be able to tell that it was made with tofu. But here's the catch—make sure you're using silken tofu, because its smooth texture results in a velvety consistency that you just cannot obtain using regular tofu. Finish the dessert with fresh berries, nuts, and grated chocolate and you're guaranteed a crowd-pleaser, albeit a lighter one.

Melt the chocolate in a microwave, stirring every 30 seconds or until smooth, or over a double boiler. It will only take a few minutes. Next, add all of the ingredients (except the garnish) into a blender or food processor and blitz until the mixture is velvety and resembles a chocolate milkshake. Pour the mixture into a bowl or into small cups/jars.

Chill for 30 minutes to an hour or until the puddings have set; the longer you chill them, the firmer they will become. Enjoy cold, as it is or with some fresh fruit.

Storing: These will last just over a week if sealed and stored properly in the fridge.

Note: You can use any milk you like. I use 2 percent milk, but coconut milk is also nice, as are other non-dairy milks (just keep in mind that one with a strong flavor may alter the taste of the mousse).

No-Bake Raw, Vegan Brownies

Prep time: 20 min

Cook time: 1–2 min

Makes: 16–25 pieces

For the "brownies":

225 g / 7.9 oz (1 cup) soft dates (such as Medjool); should be around 175 g / 6.2 oz when pitted*

50 g / 1.8 oz (½ cup) unsalted walnuts*

75 g / 2.6 oz (½ cup) unsalted almonds*

30 g / 1.1 oz (6 tablespoons) raw cacao powder or cocoa powder

1 tablespoon chia seeds (optional)

½ teaspoon salt

2–4 tablespoons whole almonds, roughly chopped (for crunch) + more for garnish (optional)

For the topping:

2 tablespoons raw cacao powder or cocoa powder

2 tablespoons coconut oil, melted

1 tablespoon agave nectar or any other sweetener (for a sweeter ganache, use 2 tablespoons of syrup)

Recently, my Pinterest account has been plagued with vegan brownies that replace butter with puréed avocado, black beans (yes, black beans) or sweet potato. "The *best* brownies," the captions read. "You can't even taste the vegetables!" But in many cases, you can (at least in my experience), and they just don't taste like brownies. This recipe is the exception. Made with chia seeds, dates, and walnuts, you'll end up with rich, chocolatey, chewy delights.

To make the "brownies," cover a large plate or board with greaseproof baking paper or a piece of greased foil. You can alternatively use a 23 x 13 cm (9 x 5 inch) loaf tin that has been greased and lined with parchment. Set aside.

Next, pit the dates by slicing them in half and removing the seeds. To your food processor, add your nuts, cacao powder or cocoa powder, chia seeds, and salt. Blitz the ingredients until you're left with a mixture that resembles sand. Add the dates and continue to blitz until the mixture comes together in a ball. If you find that the mixture is too dry, you can add a date or two more. If you find the mixture too sticky, blitz up a couple more nuts and add to the date-nut mixture, until you are able to touch the dough without it sticking to your fingers.

Spoon the dough out onto the prepared tray and press it into a large square about half an inch thick.* Press the 2 to 4 tablespoons of extra roughly chopped almonds into the square and let it chill in the fridge while making the topping.

To make the topping, combine the cacao powder/cocoa powder, the melted coconut oil, and the agave nectar until your result is a moderately thin, glossy glaze. Let the topping harden in the fridge or at room temperature, stirring every now and then, until it resembles a thick chocolate frosting. If it firms up too much, you can place it in the microwave for about 5 seconds and then stir to combine. Spread the topping on the raw brownie square and garnish with more almonds. Cut the brownie into 16 to 25 pieces (these are rich, and a little goes a long way).

Storing: These bars can be stored in an airtight container at room temperature for 2 weeks, and last about a month in the fridge.

Notes:

♦ If you can only find dry dates, soak them in boiling hot water for about 10 minutes, until soft, before using.

♦ I use half walnuts, half almonds, but feel free to use any nut you like as long as it amounts to a cup.

♦ You could also roll the mixture into balls and coat with cacao powder or coconut flakes to create energy bites.

Chia Seed Pudding: Two Delicious Ways

Prep time: 15 min

Cook time: None!

Makes: 4–6 servings (per recipe)

For the chocolate chia seed pudding:

400 mL / 13.5 fl oz (1 can) coconut milk

50–75 mL / 1.7–2.5 fl oz (4–5
  tablespoons) maple syrup/agave
  nectar, depending on how sweet
  you like it

100 g / 3.5 oz (½ cup) chia seeds

25 g / 0.9 oz (¼ cup) cocoa powder

½ teaspoon ground cinnamon

Fresh fruit to serve

**For the breakfast vanilla chia
seed pudding:**

500 mL / 16.9 fl oz (2 cups) milk of
  your choice, such as almond milk,
  coconut milk from a carton, regular
  milk, etc.

1 tablespoon maple syrup or honey
  (optional)

100 g / 3.5 oz (½ cup) chia seeds

½ teaspoon ground cinnamon

½ teaspoon vanilla extract (optional)

Fresh fruit to serve

Chia seeds are nutritionally dense flecks that thicken up any liquid you choose to combine them with, making them a slightly more interesting way to change up your breakfast routine or even your dessert options. I'm sharing with you two varieties of chia seed pudding: the first is a rich, chocolatey version that is slightly more appropriate as a dessert. The second is one that I like to make the night before, sometimes with oats, and enjoy for breakfast the next morning with some fruit. Whichever variety you choose, your decision to try this recipe is a wise one.

Whether you are making the chocolate variety or the breakfast variety, place the ingredients (except the fresh fruit) into a bowl and whisk until smooth. Pour the mixture into an airtight container.

Chill the pudding in the refrigerator for 6 hours or overnight. The pudding will continue to thicken the longer you leave it in the fridge. Then you can spoon it into small jars or ramekins and serve with the fruit.

Storing: The pudding keeps for about five days in the fridge, sealed properly, without the fruit. Right before serving, give it a quick mix to loosen the mixture slightly.

Fluffy Banana and Oat Pancakes

Prep time: 10 minutes

Cook time: 10–15 minutes

Makes: 10–12 pancakes

Ingredients

150 g / 5.3 oz (1 cup) whole wheat flour

2 teaspoons baking powder

50 g / 1.8 oz (½ cup) rolled oats

Pinch of salt

1 teaspoon ground cinnamon

1 tablespoon sugar or honey (optional)*

250 mL / 8.5 fl oz (1 cup) milk*

1 tablespoon plain or apple
  cider vinegar

1 medium-sized ripe banana (the one
  with the most little brown spots),
  mashed (approx. 120 g / 4.2 oz
  or ½ cup)*

1 tsp vanilla extract

1–2 tablespoons oil (or butter for an
  extra indulgent treat!) for cooking

Fruit and syrup to serve*

I present you with these important banana and oat pancakes, fit for the most important meal of the day. These are fluffy, sweetened with a ripened banana, and jazzed up with a touch of oats for a slight bite. Healthier than your average pancake, you can compensate by dousing them in copious amounts of maple syrup. Your call.

In a large bowl, gently stir together the flour, baking powder, oats, salt, cinnamon, and honey or sugar, then set aside. In another, smaller bowl, stir together the milk and vinegar. It will clump slightly—that's fine! This combination makes the pancakes soft and fluffy. Add the mashed banana (it is important to use a ripe banana, since it adds sweetness and moisture to the pancake) to the milk mixture, followed by the vanilla. Add the milk-banana mixture to the flour mixture, and stir gently, just until combined. Overmixing will result in a tougher pancake. If the mixture is too thick for your liking, you can add some more milk. Additionally, use a spatula to scrape down the bottom of the bowl, to make sure all the flour is well-incorporated.

Place a large non-stick frying pan on the stovetop and let it heat up with a dash of oil (or butter). I actually like to prepare the pancake batter while the pan is heating up, since it takes a few minutes. When the pan is hot, turn the heat to medium low and scoop around 60 mL / 2 fl oz (¼ cup) of the batter into the pan. I fry around 2 to 3 at a time—just make sure they don't stick together.

Cook the pancakes until bubbles begin to appear on the surface—this might take a minute or two. At that point, flip the pancake over, and let it cook for a minute or so or until it's cooked through, which will take around two minutes. You'll need to play around with the temperature of the pan: if the pancakes are browning too quickly, reduce the heat. Just make sure to watch the pancakes closely; you'll get the hang of it after the first few.

Serve them immediately, with fresh fruit (I like bananas and berries), syrup, and perhaps some butter if you are feeling indulgent.

Storing: These are best served immediately after making.

Notes:

♦ The sugar or honey is for a little extra sweetness but can be left out.

♦ Vinegar and milk can be replaced with buttermilk, or a combination of yogurt and milk (use 1 part yogurt and 3 parts milk).

♦ The banana can be replaced with applesauce, but you might need a bit of sugar or syrup to sweeten it. You could also add in some chopped nuts, or blueberries if you like.

Grab 'n' Go Peanut Butter and Date Energy Bites

Prep time: 15–20 min

Cook time: 8–10 min

Makes: approximately 18 pieces

Ingredients

125 g / 4.4 oz (1 cup) whole rolled oats (can also replace with instant oats)

150 g / 5.3 oz (1 cup) unsalted almonds (walnuts or peanuts are also nice—any nut works!), roughly chopped

Handful of flax seeds (1–2 tablespoons)

Handful of sunflower seeds (1–2 tablespoons)

175 g / 6.2 oz (1 cup) soft, pitted, and packed dates (such as Medjool)*

75 g / 2.6 oz (around ¼ cup) natural peanut butter* (any nut butter, such as almond or cashew, will also work)

½ teaspoon ground cinnamon

A pinch of salt

½ tablespoon chia seeds

Drizzle of honey (optional)

Filled with wholesome ingredients, this recipe gives you a healthier option when it comes to satisfying your sweet tooth. These energy bites are packed with natural sugar, spice, and all things nice and are an excellent source of protein. The Medjool dates in this recipe are key, as they not only act as a binding agent, but also bring sweetness and lend a slight caramel flavor to this tasty treat. You could also try this recipe with raisins, prunes, or dried apricots (see the note below the recipe). As long as you have the dates and oats, the rest of the ingredients are relatively easy to switch out with what you have available. This is the version that I most frequently refer back to though. Each time I visit home, I usually prepare a box or two of these, one for my family and one to take back with me. They make a great on-the-go snack, and I often pack them to munch on between lectures.

In a food processor, lightly pulse the oats* (unless you are using quick cooking oats—then you can skip this step). The oats should still be coarse, but slightly finer than rolled oats. This helps reduce the chew that the oatmeal lends.

Optional step: Next, toast the ingredients. Toasting the oats takes these energy balls to the next level and gives them a nice crunch. To do this, preheat the oven to 180°C (350°F) and line a baking tray with parchment paper. Place the oats, almonds (or other nut variety), flax seeds, and sunflower seeds on the tray in a single layer. Bake them for around 8 to 10 minutes or until lightly golden brown and fragrant, then set aside while you prepare the remaining ingredients.

In the meantime, place the dates in a food processor* and blitz until the mixture is thick, smooth, and creamy, and set aside. While still warm (if toasted), tip the nuts, seeds, and oats into a large bowl. Add in the peanut butter, as well as the date mixture. Combine all the remaining ingredients.* You can use a spatula or spoon to do this, but using your hands is easiest. I like to wet my hands slightly with some water, or grease them with oil to prevent sticking. You could also use cooking gloves.

The mixture will be quite sticky (fair warning). Work the mixture together till the dates are well-incorporated throughout. All the ingredients should come together, but if you find the mixture is too dry, add some honey to bind it. If it's far too sticky for your liking, add more oats. At this point, I also like to wash my hands, then scoop the mixture into 2-tablespoon-sized mounds to form balls. Clean hands make it easy to bring together.

Keep going till you've used up all the mixture.

Storing: Store the balls in an airtight container, at room temperature or in the fridge. These last for several weeks if stored properly.

Notes:

- If the dates are too dry, you can soak them in hot water before blending. You can also replace the dates with other plump dried fruit, such as apricots, prunes, figs, or raisins. However, note that you may need to soak them before using since raisins, for instance, tend to be much drier.

- If you use regular peanut butter, you may need to warm it so that it is easier to work with.

- If you don't have a food processor, you can try mashing the dates with a fork, but they will need to be quite soft. You can also try crushing them using a mortar and pestle. You can also use instant oats instead of whole rolled oats, and then you won't need the food processor at all.

- You could also throw in some cocoa powder for a bit of a chocolatey flavor. You can also add desiccated coconut or whatever you like—just keep in mind the texture.

Morning Glory Muffins

Prep time: 25–30 min

Cook time: 30–35 min

Makes: 13–15 muffins

Ingredients

280 g / 9.9 oz (2 cups) all-purpose flour*

250 g / 8.8 oz (1¼ cup) cup granulated sugar*

2 teaspoons baking soda

2 teaspoons cinnamon

½ teaspoon salt

280 g / 9.9 oz (2 cups) carrots, peeled and shredded (3–4 carrots)

70 g / 2.5 oz (½ cup) raisins

70 g / 2.5 oz (½ cup) unsalted walnuts, chopped

40 g / 1.4 oz (½ cup) shredded or desiccated coconut*

1 apple, peeled, cored, grated (150 g / 5.3 oz, around 1 cup)

3 large eggs

250 mL / 8.5 fl oz (1 cup) vegetable oil*

2 teaspoons vanilla extract

This recipe comes from my friend and fellow food enthusiast, Noah, who got it from his mother, who got it from his grandmother, who got it from his great-grandmother. Noah would frequently mention these muffins, praising everything about them and eventually he shared an index card with a handwritten version of the recipe, courtesy of his grandmother. When I tried the recipe, I liked it so much that I instantly wrote to him, asking whether I could include it in this book. At the bottom of this recipe, you can also find my own notes, some of them to make these slightly healthier for this time of year. Either way, you're in for a glorious treat, perfect with your morning tea or coffee.

First, preheat the oven to 180°C or 350°F, and prepare the muffin trays by lining them with paper liners. You'll need 12 to 15. Next, in a large bowl, stir together the flour, sugar, baking soda, cinnamon, and salt until well-combined. Add in the grated carrot, raisins, chopped nuts, coconut, and apple, stirring to combine.* In a separate bowl, mix together the eggs, oil, and vanilla extract.

Stir the wet ingredients into the flour mixture, scraping the bottom and sides of the bowl to make sure everything is combined. Do not overmix. Spoon the batter into the prepared liners, all the way to the top.

Bake the muffins for 30 to 35 minutes or until a toothpick inserted comes out clean.

Let the muffins cool in the tins for several minutes, then remove them and let them cool on a wire rack before enjoying.

Storing: These can be stored in an airtight container in the refrigerator for up to a week.

Notes:

♦ You can replace the white flour with whole wheat flour or use a combination of the two.

♦ Reduce the sugar by ¼ cup, and you can use coconut sugar.

♦ If you can't find shredded coconut, you can use desiccated coconut instead.

♦ To make these healthier, replace half of the oil with applesauce and use olive oil.

♦ You can also add 1 tablespoon orange zest if you like.

February

Where I live, February is the dead of winter, and with it comes low temperatures and lots of shivers. If we are lucky though, with these frigid temperatures comes snow. When the ground is blanketed in white and the lakes freeze over, excitement is buzzing, as people scurry to dig out their ice skates and sleds.

To me, the winter months mean comfort food. Food that brings a certain heartiness and warmth is sort of a necessity when the weather is cold. Chocolate, perfect for Valentine's Day, takes center stage this month. February is a great excuse to treat yourself and your loved ones to decadent confections like the recipes in this section. Salted Caramel Whiskey Truffles and Brown Butter and Pecan Chocolate Chip Cookies not only make great gifts, but are decadent, chocolatey, and purely delicious. If you're feeling extra indulgent, you can try the Flourless Chocolate Cake, served with whipped cream and raspberry coulis (puree). This cake is delicious for all occasions; rich, velvety, and sure to win you bonus points on Valentine's Day. Next, we have the delicate Baklava-inspired palmiers, the heart-shaped treats that are also on the cover. Lastly, we have *Pączki* or Polish jelly doughnuts traditionally served on Fat Tuesday. While these last two deviate from the chocolate theme of the month, they are sure to please.

Salted Caramel Whiskey Truffles

For the truffles:

Prep time: 20 min

Cook time: 2–5 min

Makes: 16–18 (depending on how big you make them)

300 g / 10.6 oz (1¾ cups) bittersweet chocolate, roughly chopped

125 mL / 4.2 fl oz (½ cup) heavy whipping cream

125 mL / 4.2 fl oz (½ cup) salted caramel (store-bought or use the recipe below!)

3 tablespoons whiskey (optional, but highly recommended!)

50 g / 1.8 oz (¼ cup) unsalted butter, cubed

1 teaspoon instant espresso powder

1 teaspoon sea salt and more for sprinkling

Unsweetened cocoa powder (40–50 g / 1.4–1.8 oz / about ½ cup) for coating

For the caramel sauce:

Prep time: 5 min

Cook time: 15–20 min

Makes: Approx. 300 mL / 10.1 fl oz, a heaping cup

3 tablespoons water

1 tablespoon light corn syrup or maple syrup

225 g / 7.9 oz (1 cup) granulated sugar

1 tablespoon unsalted butter

190 mL / 6.4 fl oz (¾ cup) heavy whipping cream

½ to 1 teaspoon salt (or more, depending on how salty you like it)

1 teaspoon vanilla extract

I made this recipe for the first time nearly five years ago, and my sister still reminisces about it to this day—quite impressive given that she's tried countless desserts of mine, and she has insanely high standards. The whiskey and salted caramel add a delicious, unexpected kick (although this recipe is also great without them), making these truffles the perfect Valentine's Day confection or an anytime decadent sweet.

To make the truffles:

Place the chocolate in a large bowl. In a separate bowl, combine the cream, caramel, whiskey, and butter and roughly stir together. Then, heat the bowl in a microwave for 2 to 3 minutes or until boiling. Alternatively, place the ingredients in a saucepan over medium-low heat, stirring every now and then until the mixture comes to a boil.

Pour the hot cream mixture over the chopped chocolate and let the ingredients stand for 30 seconds to a minute without stirring. Next, add in the instant espresso powder and sea salt and whisk the mixture until thick, smooth, and glossy. Taste and add more salt if you feel it is necessary. Cover the bowl with plastic wrap and chill for 5 hours or overnight.

To shape the truffles, scoop 2 tablespoon-sized mounds of the mixture and sprinkle with a little cocoa. WARNING: This stuff is super messy, so either grease your hands with a little oil or dust them with cocoa powder before rolling. Roll the truffles into ball shapes and then dust with the cocoa powder. Keep the truffles chilled until ready to serve, then sprinkle with sea salt for a final garnish.

To make the caramel sauce:

In a small pan, add the water, corn syrup, and sugar. Then stir just enough to combine.

Place the pan over medium heat without stirring—you can swirl the pan. To prevent sugar crystals from forming on the sides, dip a brush in some water and gently brush off the sides until the crystals are gone.

As soon as the caramel becomes a bubbly amber color, turn off the heat. This should take 5 to 7 minutes. Be careful not to overcook, as burnt caramel is not tasty.

Stand back (this is known to splatter) and add the butter and heavy whipping cream. When the mixture calms down slightly, stir the ingredients until the sauce is silky smooth.

Add the salt and vanilla and stir to taste. Start by adding ½ teaspoon salt, and then add more if you like. I always add a touch more!

Storing: The truffles last about two weeks in the fridge, and the sauce does too if cooled and sealed properly.

Brown Butter Pecan Chocolate Chip Cookies with Sea Salt

Prep time: 20 min

Cook time: 9–10 min

Makes: roughly 18

Ingredients

115 g / 4.1 oz (½ cup) unsalted butter

90 g / 3.2 oz (½ cup) brown sugar

60 g / 2.1 oz (¼ cup) granulated sugar

1 large egg

1 teaspoon vanilla extract

1 teaspoon salt

½ teaspoon baking soda

190 g / 6.7 oz (1¼ cups) all-purpose flour

100 g / 3.5 oz (½ cup) unsalted pecans, chopped

150–200 g / 5.3–7.1 oz (around ¾ to 1 heaping cup) dark chocolate (60–70 percent cacao solids), roughly chopped (the amount of chocolate depends on your flavor preference)

flaked sea salt for garnishing

Cookie-baking is an art, but not one that is difficult to master. The perfect cookie has a crisp exterior, a soft, chewy interior, a light saltiness, and just the right amount of chocolate. It took me ten years to find and perfect my favorite recipe, and I am excited to share it with you. This cookie's outrageous flavor is enhanced using brown butter, which adds a layer of depth. I also throw in chopped pecans for a a little crunch, delicate texture, and flavor. Trust me, a batch of fresh chocolate chip cookies will win over even the most anti-holiday grouchy souls out there.

Add the butter to a small saucepan and let it melt over medium heat, until it comes to a boil. Swirl the pan occasionally until brown flecks begin to appear on the surface of the butter, and the liquid begins to turn an amber color. It should give off a nutty, caramel-like aroma after about 5 to 8 minutes. It is better to undercook rather than overcook the butter, since it goes from brown to burnt quickly once it reaches the right color.

Take the butter off the heat and pour it into a bowl, then let it cool to room temperature.

Add the brown sugar and granulated sugar to the butter, followed by the egg and vanilla extract. Once you add the egg, the mixture should thicken. Next, stir in the salt, baking soda, and flour and stir until well-incorporated. Finally, fold in the nuts and chocolate chunks.

Cover the bowl with plastic wrap and chill in the refrigerator for at least 30 minutes or up to 2 days. Chilling the dough makes the flavors more prominent and makes it easier to shape the cookies. In the meantime, preheat the oven to 180°C (350°F) and line a baking tray with parchment paper.

Roll the dough into 1½-tablespoon-sized balls and place about 2 inches apart on the tray.

Bake for 9 to 10 minutes or until the edges are golden and the center is just set.

If anything, I prefer under-baking the cookies by a minute rather than over-baking them. This ensures they are chewier and softer, rather than crispier. Sprinkle the cookies with flaky sea salt if using, then let them cool for 5 minutes. Transfer to a plate and enjoy.

Storing: The cookies store well for up to 2 weeks when sealed properly at room temperature.

Tip: To keep your cookies soft, store them with a slice of bread overnight they will soften up as they absorb the moisture.

Flourless Chocolate Cake with Raspberry Coulis

Prep time: 30 min

Baking time: 45 min

Makes: 8–10 servings

For the cake

350 g / 12.3 oz (2 cups) dark chocolate, around 60 percent cacao solids

150 g / 5.3 oz (¾ cup) unsalted butter

4 large eggs

125 g / 4.4 oz (⅔ cup) granulated sugar (you can reduce the sugar if you like a more intense cake)

½ teaspoon salt

For the raspberry coulis:

250 g / 8.8 oz fresh or frozen raspberries

2 tablespoons granulated sugar, or to taste

Lemon juice, to taste

People associate allergen-friendly desserts with foods devoid of taste, which isn't at all the case here. This cake is velvety smooth, incredibly rich and fudgey, piled with freshly whipped cream and swirled with raspberry sauce—a fundamental component of this recipe. If you like chocolate, you'll love this cake, gluten-intolerant or not.

First, preheat the oven to 180°C or 350°F. Next, generously butter a 22-cm (9-inch) round cake pan, line the bottom with parchment paper, and dust the sides with cocoa powder. Set aside.

To make the cake, melt the chocolate and butter over a double boiler on a low flame (or in the microwave, stirring every 20 to 30 seconds until smooth). Let the chocolate cool.

In the meantime, using an electric mixer, beat the eggs with sugar and salt until pale, fluffy, and significantly larger in volume. The mixture should form a ribbon when you lift the beaters up.

Add around ⅓ of the egg mixture to the chocolate to lighten it up. Next, gently fold the chocolate mixture into the remaining egg mixture, being careful not to deflate the eggs.

Pour the batter into the prepared cake tin. Place the tin in a larger oven dish, such as a roasting dish, and pour boiling water into the larger dish so that the cake is surrounded by a hot water bath that comes up to about ¾ of the depth the cake pan. Be careful to ensure that the water does not enter the cake pan itself. Place the cake dish in the hot water bath in the oven.

Bake the cake for 45 minutes. A toothpick inserted will not come out completely clean even when the baking time is done, but this is fine. Remove the cake from the oven, let it cool to room temperature, then cover it and chill for several hours or until cold.

To prepare the raspberry sauce:

Combine the raspberries with the sugar in a food processor and blend until smooth. Taste it, adding more sugar and/or lemon juice until you are happy with the flavor. Strain the raspberry sauce through a fine-mesh sieve until all that's left are the seeds. This step is optional but it results in a smoother sauce.

Serve the cake with whipped cream and raspberry coulis.

Storing: The cake will last up to a week if sealed properly in the fridge. Serve immediately once you prepare the cream and fruit.

Baklava-Inspired Palmiers (Elephant Ears)

Prep time: 20 min

Baking time: 15–20 min

Makes: Around 30

Ingredients

50 g / 1.8 oz (½ cup) unsalted walnuts

50 g / 1.8 oz (½ cup) unsalted
pistachios, shelled

50 g / 1.8 oz (¼ cup) unsalted butter

1 teaspoon ground cinnamon

½ teaspoon ground cardamom

A pinch of salt

2 tablespoons brown sugar

300 g / 10.6 oz puff pastry

125 mL / 4.2 fl oz (½ cup)
honey, warmed

This is my simplified version of a classic Middle Eastern delicacy. It is a fragrant mix of pastry, nuts, and honey that is impossible to resist. This is by no means a traditional recipe, but it does have many of the same ingredients as a traditional baklava, and my family loves it. This tasty treat also comes together in minutes. The shape of the palmiers makes them perfect for the month of February: they look like little hearts and make a lovely teatime treat or present.

First, preheat the oven to 180°C or 350°F. Finely crush the walnuts and pistachios—I like to do this using a mortar and pestle, but you could also finely chop the nuts. I wouldn't recommend using a food processor since it is nice to have some texture. In a small bowl, add the butter, followed by the cinnamon, cardamom, salt, nuts, and brown sugar. The mixture should form a nice paste.

Next, roll out the puff pastry in an even, rectangular layer, then spread the nut mixture on top and to the sides. Firmly roll the pastry from both of the long sides until the two rolls meet in the middle, then press them together.

Using a serrated knife, slice the dough into half-cm (quarter-inch) slices, to yield about 20 pieces.

Bake the cookies for 15 to 20 minutes or until golden brown, and let them cool for a few minutes. While the cookies are still warm, brush them with the honey.

Let the cookies cool completely, then brush again with the honey.

Storing: These keep well for up to a week, stored in an airtight container at room temperature.

Pączki (Jelly Doughnuts)

Prep time: 30 min (excluding rising)

Cooking time: 15 min

Makes: 8–10 doughnuts (double the recipe to make more)

Ingredients

150 mL / 5.1 fl oz (10 tablespoons) milk

2 tablespoons granulated sugar

1½ teaspoons active dry yeast or instant yeast

50 g / 1.8 oz (¼ cup) unsalted butter, melted

1 large egg

½ teaspoon salt

1 teaspoon vanilla extract

375 g / 13.2 oz (2 ¾ cups) all-purpose flour

500 mL / 16.9 fl oz (2 cups) flavorless oil for frying (i.e., canola or vegetable)

165 g / 5.8 oz (10 tablespoons) strawberry jam (or any other jam of choice)*

Confectioners' sugar, for dusting

Fat Thursday marks the last Thursday before Lent, a Christian occasion that marks a time of fasting. In Poland, Fat Thursday means a feast of confections, including the traditional *pączki*, or jelly doughnuts. Festivities were present even in my high school, where the cafeteria would serve fluffy *pączki*, filled with strawberry jam, either dusted in confectioners' sugar or dipped in a sweet glaze, the highlight of our lunch break. The recipe is one that can be used to make virtually any doughnut, whether you prefer a classic glazed variety or something more extravagant. This *pączki* recipe is a crowd-pleaser every time.

Pour the milk into a medium-sized bowl. Heat it up in the microwave for around 10 seconds. It should be warm, around 30–40°C (80–105°F); use a food thermometer to check.

Next, sprinkle in 2 tablespoons of granulated sugar, followed by the yeast. Give the mixture a quick stir and let it sit for around five minutes.

Next, whisk in the melted butter, egg, salt, and vanilla extract. The mixture might look a little lumpy, but it will come together once the rest of the ingredients are added.

Spoon in the flour; you'll want to do this a little bit at a time, as it makes it easier to incorporate. The resulting dough should be thick and soft and should pull away slightly from the bowl. If it's too sticky, add some more flour, but don't go overboard, as it will dry out the dough and result in a tougher doughnut. Work the dough on a dry surface for around two minutes, until it comes together in a nice ball. Place the dough into a bowl that has been lightly greased with some oil or butter. Then, brush the top of the dough with some oil as well, to prevent a skin from forming. Cover the bowl with a piece of plastic wrap and leave it in a relatively warm environment (if it's too cold inside, see the tip at the bottom of the recipe) until it's doubled in size. This normally takes around an hour and can take up to two hours. If you'd like to make these in advance, you can also place the bowl in the fridge and let it rise overnight.

When it's risen nicely, lightly flour a work surface and gently remove the dough from the bowl. Roll it out to about a half-inch or 1-cm thickness. Then, cut out the doughnuts using a greased cookie cutter, making each around 5 cm (2.5–3 inches) in diameter. You can also use a drinking glass if you don't have a cookie cutter in this size; just make sure it's greased. *Note that if you want regular doughnuts, you can also cut a little hole out of the center of the circle using a smaller cookie cutter or bottle cap.

You can make smaller doughnuts too! This is a great all-around recipe. Bunch the scraps together and roll them out once more, being careful not to add too much extra flour.

Gently place the little rounds onto a lightly floured surface, around 2 cm (1 inch) apart. Cover them with a tea towel. Let the doughnuts rise again for around an hour, or until they have puffed up and nearly doubled. Then you're ready to fry! To fry the doughnuts, heat the oil in a medium-sized pot. I recommend starting this around five minutes before you intend to fry. The oil should be hot, about 190°C, or 375°F, if you check using a food thermometer. You can see whether it's hot enough by placing a small scrap of the dough in it: if the oil begins to bubble around the edges of the dough, and the dough emerges on the surface and turns a light golden brown, it's done.

While the oil is heating up, line a plate or tray with paper towels and set aside.

Gently place a risen doughnut in the oil, being careful not to deflate it. Use a metal slotted spoon to do this. Note that you really need to monitor the temperature of the oil. If it's too hot, the doughnut will be well-browned within seconds, but the inside will be doughy and raw. When the temperature is right, cook a few at a time, for around a minute on each side, or until they've developed a nice golden-brown color and have puffed up. Next, slide the doughnuts onto a paper-towel-lined plate so that the excess oil can drain off.

Once you've fried all the doughnuts, you can fill them with the jam. The best way to do this is using a piping bag and a nozzle, but you can also cut the doughnut in half and spread the jam inside. If you're using a piping bag and nozzle (I use a small, #10 nozzle), make sure the jam isn't too lumpy (either strain it or puree it in the blender before using, to remove lumps). Otherwise, pieces of fruit may get trapped in the piping bag and prevent you from squeezing.

Make an indent on the side of each doughnut using the nozzle. Make sure to do this on the side of the doughnut and not on the top or bottom. Then place the nozzle into the piping bag with the end snipped off. Pour the jam into the piping bag, and squeeze into the indent you made earlier, just gently. You only want each doughnut to hold about a tablespoon of jam. Generously dust the doughnuts with the confectioners' sugar before serving.

Storing: These are best served while they are still warm. The dough itself can be stored overnight, covered in the fridge. However, these doughnuts must be eaten fresh, as the longer you wait, the more stale they will go, so make sure to fry them right before eating.

Note: Instead of making filled doughnuts, you can also make a classic American doughnut by cutting out a small circle of the larger circle before frying. This also helps the doughnut cook more easily and you will also have smaller doughnut "holes" to fry.

Tip: Where to let the dough rise. If it's too cold indoors, make your own warm environment to help the dough rise. To do this, preheat your oven to 65°C or 150°F. Once it reaches that temperature, turn off the heat, wait several minutes, and place the bowl of dough inside the oven with the oven door slightly open. Let the dough rise for 30 minutes, then close the oven door to trap the warm air and let it rise for the specified duration of time.

March

March signifies a revival. Small leaves sprout from bare branches, and in the early morning, if you listen carefully, you can hear the birds chirp. Don't let the gentle weather fool you though, as one day it may snow, the next day thunder, and the day after, everyone is outside with no coats, as if it were summer. This is spring. A part of me feels nostalgic: I cherish the winter months when the landscape is painted white, the snow like glitter, and the hats, blankets, and scarves that accompany them. But I can't seem to get enough of the spring sun, which feels like nourishment to me.

March is therefore an appropriate transition month between seasons. Although the weather begins to change, the winter attire doesn't need to be put away just yet. Fittingly, this section of the book showcases a recipe for Decadent Hot Chocolate, perfect for the month not only because of the cold, but also because I like to infuse it with Irish cream, making it a perfect St. Patrick's Day treat. My Chocolate Stout Cake is also appropriate for the occasion but is really a star recipe for any time of year: a moist, sumptuous chocolate cake topped with brown butter-infused cream cheese frosting. Of course, in the spirit of spring and all things fresh, the March menu also includes a to-die-for No-Bake Biscuit and Citrus Slice recipe—an easy and refreshing treat. And finally, my favorite: Walnut and Lemon Thumbprint Cookies. These dainty confections breathe spring, make for the perfect teatime treat and are a wonderful prelude to Easter.

Decadent Hot Chocolate

Prep time: 5 min

Cook time: 5–10 min

Makes: 3–4 portions

Ingredients

125 g / 4.4 oz good-quality chocolate (you can use milk, dark, or a combination, I use half and half)*

2 teaspoons cornstarch*

Pinch of salt

½ teaspoon instant espresso powder (optional)

500–750 mL / 16.9–25.4 fl oz (2–3 cups) whole milk (depending on how rich you like your hot chocolate; I tend to use around 600 mL / 20.3 fl oz)*

Whipped cream and/or marshmallows for topping (optional)*

As my blog is called *Hot Chocolate Hits*, a recipe for hot chocolate in this cookbook is a necessity. And this is not your average hot cocoa. It is luxuriously silky and rich, more like a dessert than a drink, the kind of hot chocolate you could order at a fancy chocolate shop, warming, comforting, and satisfying. The recipe is ridiculously easy and fun to play around with. I like to infuse it with a hint of coffee, which enhances the flavor of chocolate, and for St. Patrick's Day, I also add in a touch of Irish cream. This also works wonderfully with a variety of additions, such as peppermint extract, orange zest, or rum, but can also be delicious as is.

Roughly chop the chocolate, then set aside. To a small pot, add the cornstarch, salt, and, if using, instant espresso powder, and whisk to combine. Slowly whisk in 500 mL / 16.9 fl oz (2 cups) of the milk to the cornstarch mixture. Start by adding in two tablespoons of the milk, making sure the cornstarch is completely mixed in, then add in the rest. You'll need to make sure the cornstarch is completely blended into the milk, so add the milk gradually. The mixture should be smooth, with no lumps. Turn on the heat, and bring the milk to a simmer, stirring slowly but constantly. When bubbles begin to appear on the surface, remove the pot from the heat and add the chopped chocolate. Let the mixture sit for around 30 seconds, then, using a whisk, stir the chocolate mixture until completely smooth. This is the base.

When you're ready to serve, place the pot on low heat, and let the hot chocolate mixture slowly warm up until bubbles begin to appear around the edges. At this point, switch off the heat. Pour the hot chocolate into serving glasses and enjoy with whipped cream and marshmallows.

Storing: You can either store this covered in the fridge for a day or two, or you can serve it immediately.

- Good-quality chocolate is necessary because there are very few ingredients that go into it. If you want a nice taste, it's vital to use a chocolate that you enjoy eating plain. I don't add any extra sugar to this; instead I prefer to use a combination of milk and dark chocolate.

- The cornstarch thickens the hot chocolate, making it richer. However, if you don't have any, it will work fine too; the texture will be slightly thinner, but still decadent and creamy.

- You can substitute whole milk with an alternative such as almond milk, hazelnut milk, or coconut milk for a vegan version.

- You can make your own whipped cream (see the Eton Mess, for instance, p. 107) or you can buy ready-made whipped topping.

Variations:

Irish Cream Hot Chocolate:
Add 1 tablespoon of Bailey's Irish Cream to each cup right before serving.

Orange Hot Chocolate:
Add 1 tablespoon of orange zest to the milk mixture, and follow the recipe as instructed. Strain the hot chocolate before enjoying.

Spiced Hot Chocolate:
Add ¼ teaspoon ground cinnamon and ⅛ teaspoon of cayenne pepper to the base.

Chocolate Stout Cake with Brown Butter Cream Cheese Frosting

Prep time: 30 min

Cook time: 1 hour

Makes: 8–10 slices

For the cake:

300 g / 10.6 oz (2 cups) all-purpose flour

1 teaspoon salt

2 teaspoons baking soda

1 teaspoon baking powder

500 mL / 16.9 fl oz (2 cups) dark stout, such as Guinness

125 g / 4.4 oz (½ cup) butter, cubed (you can also replace this with oil)

100 g / 3.5 oz (1 cup) unsweetened cocoa powder

400 g / 14.1 oz (2 cups) granulated sugar

1 tablespoon vinegar

For the cream cheese frosting:

50 g / 1.8 oz (¼ cup) unsalted butter

125 g / 4.4 oz (½ cup) cream cheese, cold from the fridge

250 g / 8.8 oz (2 cups) confectioners' sugar

1 teaspoon vanilla extract

2 teaspoons lemon juice (optional)

Pinch of salt

This recipe gives everything one could possibly want in a chocolate cake and more, and yet the star ingredient isn't just chocolate; it's also stout beer. Yes, perhaps an odd ingredient for a dessert, but hear me out: the stout adds an earthy undertone that enhances the flavor of the chocolate more than anything else and adds a bit of flair. It's also perfect for St. Patrick's Day, which takes place in March. While I have a version of a stout chocolate cake on the blog, this recipe is new and improved, making for a devilishly dark and rich chocolate cake, enhanced by the stout (you also can replace the stout with hot water or coffee for an alcohol-free alternative). The frosting has a nutty caramel flavor, courtesy of the brown butter, which works wonders for this dessert. This cake has actually won an auction, it's so good. And a little bonus is that it doesn't require eggs.

To make the cake, preheat the oven to 180°C or 350°F and grease a 24–26 cm (9–10 inch) springform cake tin with butter. Line the base with parchment paper and then dust the tin with some cocoa powder. Make sure that the springform cake tin doesn't leak, since the batter may be quite thin—you can wrap foil around the bottom of the tin to prevent this if it does. You'll need a cake tin that is fairly tall, since this makes a lot of cake batter. You can also use a 20x30-cm (8x12 or even a 9x13-inch) rectangular pan, or something of a similar size.

In a small bowl, stir together the flour, salt, baking soda, and baking powder till combined, then set aside. In a large pot, combine the stout and butter, stirring until the butter has completely melted. Next, whisk in the cocoa powder and sugar, until the mixture is smooth. I like to combine everything in the pot itself, but you can also transfer the ingredients to a separate bowl.

Then, add the vinegar to this mixture. Next, slowly add in the flour mixture to the liquid. Note that the mixture might bubble and foam, since there's quite a lot of acid-base reaction going on, so make sure your pot is large enough to accommodate this.

Pour the batter into your prepared tin. It might look foamy, but don't worry, it will settle as it bakes. Bake the cake for 45 to 50 minutes, or until a toothpick inserted comes out clean. Let the cake cool completely before frosting.

For the frosting, place the butter in a small saucepan or pot over medium heat and let it melt. Swirl the pan every now and then. The butter will begin to boil and crackle. When it starts to turn a light golden color, and releases a nutty aroma, take the pot off the heat. This will take around 5 to 8 minutes.

Pour the butter into a large heatproof bowl and let it cool completely (you can pop it in the fridge to help speed things up). Add the cream cheese, whisking till well-blended. Next, beat in the confectioners' sugar, mixing a little bit at a time, until the icing is smooth and thick. Finally, whisk in the vanilla extract, salt and lemon, juice if using. Taste the icing, and add more lemon juice, vanilla extract or salt if you think it is necessary. Cream cheese icing is delicious; however, it is not, in my experience, the best for piping, as it tends to be thinner than buttercream, so proceed with caution. I like to lather a single layer of the frosting atop the cake, and using a butter knife, I make small swirls. For stiffer frosting, be sure to chill the frosting well before spreading.

Storing: This cake keeps for around a week, if sealed properly and stored in the fridge (but I doubt it will last that long, because your friends and housemates will be clamoring for more).

No-Bake Biscuit and Citrus Slice

Prep time: 25 min

Cook time: 5 min

Makes: 12–16 squares

For the base:

250 g / 8.8 oz tea biscuits, crushed (should amount to 2½ cups)

1 tablespoon lemon, lime, or orange zest (or a combination!)

½ teaspoon salt

90 g / 3.2 oz (1 cup) desiccated coconut

175 g / 6.2 oz (½ cup) sweetened condensed milk

115 g / 4.1 oz (½ cup) unsalted butter

For the icing:

225 g / 7.9 oz (1¾ cups) confectioners' sugar

25 g / 0.9 oz (2 tablespoons) unsalted butter, melted

3 tablespoons freshly squeezed lemon, lime, or orange juice (or a combination!)

1 teaspoon lemon, lime, or orange zest

Pinch of salt

In many desserts, it is not the filling but the crust that sets it apart, the crisp texture and gentle flavor that brings balance to the more exciting main flavor. This recipe uses the elements of a crust but makes it the star of the show rather than the supporting actor. Envision a crisp base with citrus notes and a hint of coconut, topped with a sweet citrusy glaze. I prefer to use lemons or limes in this recipe, since the tart flavor cuts through the sweetness slightly, but orange juice works fine too, and a combination of both is even better.

To make the bars, first grease a 20-to-22-cm (8-to-9-inch) square tin with some butter or oil, then line the base and sides with parchment paper (the butter helps the parchment paper stick). You can also line the pan with a piece of foil, then grease the foil with some melted butter instead.

In a large bowl, mix together the biscuit crumbs, zest, salt, and desiccated coconut. In a small saucepan or pot, combine the condensed milk and butter. Stir the ingredients together over low heat, until the butter has completely melted and the ingredients are well-combined. This will take a few minutes. Add the butter and condensed milk mixture to the biscuit mixture, and stir together gently. The mixture will be thick and resemble wet sand. Press the biscuit mixture into the prepared tin, and chill in the fridge for 1½ to 2 hours or until it is firm.

In the meantime, prepare the icing. Sift the confectioners' sugar into a bowl, then pour in the melted butter, citrus juice, zest, and salt. Whisk until thick and smooth. Spread the icing over the biscuit mixture, then chill again for 30 minutes before serving. To serve, slice into bars or squares.

Storing: These last for a week or slightly longer, if stored properly in the fridge.

Dainty Walnut and Lemon Thumbprint Cookies

Prep time: 30 min

Cook time: 15 min

Makes: 30–36 cookies

For the shortbread:

225 g / 7.9 oz (1 cup) unsalted butter, softened at room temperature

75 g / 2.6 oz (½ cup) confectioners' sugar

100 g / 3.5 oz (1 cup) unsalted walnuts, finely chopped*

1 teaspoon vanilla extract

½ teaspoon salt

300 g / 10.6 oz (2¼ cups) all-purpose flour

For the lemon curd:

120 g / 4.2 oz (½ cup) granulated sugar

2 large eggs

120 mL / 4.1 fl oz (½ cup) freshly squeezed lemon juice (juice of 3–4 lemons)

Pinch of salt

60 g / 2.1 oz (¼ cup) unsalted butter, cut into 1-cm (half-inch) cubes

This buttery, walnut-speckled shortbread cookie is filled with a silky smooth, tart lemon curd. The lemon curd is not only perfect for this particular recipe, but also goes well with many other desserts (Lime and Coconut Cake, p. 81, Victoria Sponge Cake, p. 113). This cookie is a simpler version of a lemon meringue pie: a miniature and far easier confection to prepare at home, with friends and family. Children will love pressing the cookie dough to create the indent and spooning the lemon filling into the craters. Dusted with a touch of confectioners' sugar, these gems are best described as "sunshine" and are sure to be a family favorite!

Preheat the oven to 180°C (350°F) and line a cookie sheet with parchment paper.

To prepare the cookie dough, mix together the butter, sugar, and walnuts—the result should be a thick, creamy mixture, courtesy of the softened butter. Add the vanilla extract and salt.

Next, fold in the flour. Your resulting mass should be a thick dough that can easily be rolled with your fingertips. If you find the mixture too sticky, transfer it to the freezer for 15 minutes, or the fridge for around 30 minutes, so that it has a chance to firm up slightly.

Then roll the dough into roughly 1-tablespoon to 1½-tablespoon-sized balls. Here comes the (moderately) tricky part. Place the cookie ball on the baking sheet and, using your thumb, press into the center of the ball to make an indentation. This is where the lemon curd will go. If there are cracks, just smooth them out with your fingers; the dough is very forgiving.

Bake the cookies around 3 cm apart, for 15 to 17 minutes or until the bottoms are lightly golden brown. While the cookies are baking, you can make the lemon curd.

For the lemon curd, place a small pot over medium heat, filling it with about 2 inches (4 cm) of water, and let the water come to a boil. Then reduce the flame to medium low. In a medium-sized heatproof, glass bowl, blend together the sugar, eggs, lemon juice, and pinch of salt until well-combined.

Next, add in the butter. Place the bowl over the pot with the water as it boils. It shouldn't be touching the water. Stir the mixture constantly until it thickens and resembles the consistency of a hollandaise sauce. This takes around 10 minutes after putting it on the heat. You'll be able to see light strokes of the whisk, and if you coat the back of a spoon with the mixture and run your finger down the middle of the spoon, the line should stick.

This lemon curd goes through several phases. Initially, it will look slightly clumpy as the butter melts. Then it will be quite thin, and then it thickens quite quickly—at which you can let it cook for around 1 to 2 minutes so that it thickens a bit more. Turn off the heat, transfer the lemon curd to a different bowl, and let it cool slightly. If you're using the curd for another purpose, cover the top with plastic wrap (cling film) and store it in the fridge in an airtight container. If you're using it for these cookies, keep reading.

Assembling:

When the cookies are out of the oven, they will resemble little craters. If the indent is not deep enough, use the back of a teaspoon to gently press down while they are still hot, and then let them cool completely. This takes around 15 minutes. Spoon the lemon curd into each indent. I like to fill them with as much curd as possible, around 2 teaspoons.

Do this while the curd is still hot, as it makes it easier and the curd will set slightly in the cookies as they cool. You can also let the curd chill and spoon it in later, in large mounds. Let the cookies cool completely, then dust with confectioners' sugar before serving.

Storing: The lemon curd lasts for several weeks if stored properly in the fridge. The cookies store well for around two weeks in an airtight container at room temperature before adding the lemon curd. Once you add the lemon curd, it's best to store these in the fridge. They will last just about a week once filled.

Note You can replace the walnuts with any kind of nut or leave them out entirely.

April

In April, spring is in full bloom. In the Netherlands, the brightly colored tulips are at their peak, and tourists from across the world flock to see the fields of bold hues. Spring is accompanied by a fresh, positive energy, a result of the sun that lingers for longer and longer each day. For this reason, the April section of this book brings you more recipes fit for spring, such as the Lime and Coconut Cake, a festive twist on a more traditional lemon loaf cake. In keeping with the citrus theme is the Orange, Olive Oil, and Poppyseed Cake, with Macerated Strawberries. It is an intriguing spring delicacy, an unconventional yet delicious dessert that is sure to be one of your favorites. Of course, April would be incomplete without Easter recipes, and for this I provide you with two of my all-time favorites: my *Mazurek*-inspired Millionaire's Shortbread, which pays tribute to my Polish upbringing, and my friend Danika and her dad's carrot cake recipe, always a winner.

Lime and Coconut Cake

Prep time: 25 min

Cook time: 45–50 min

Makes: 1 loaf, 8-10 servings

For the cake:

225 g / 7.9 oz (1½ cups) all-
purpose flour

2 teaspoons baking powder

50 g / 1.8 oz (½ cup)
desiccated coconut

½ teaspoon salt

125 g / 4.4 oz (½ cup) unsalted butter

225 g / 7.9 oz (1 cup) granulated sugar

1 lime, zested (2 teaspoons) and juiced
(2 tablespoons)

2 large eggs (at room temperature)

1 teaspoon vanilla extract

¾ cup (180 mL / 6.1 fl oz) coconut milk

For the glaze:

2 tablespoons lime juice

100 g / 3.5 oz (¾ cup)
confectioners' sugar

Extra lime zest and desiccated
coconut for garnishing

Just because of its form and shape, a loaf cake encompasses my definition of home baking: uncomplicated, comforting, healing. This recipe is that, and more. It adds a playful twist to the much-adored lemon drizzle loaf, fusing together lime and coconut to welcome the warm weather. It's a refreshing cake that works well for Easter and other spring holidays, and it's a perfect go-to for the warm summer months and gatherings to follow.

Preheat the oven to 180°C or 350°F and grease a loaf tin around 21x11 cm (9x5 inches) with butter, then line the sides with parchment paper to prevent sticking. You can also use a loaf liner (my personal favorite).

To make the cake batter, in a medium-sized bowl, mix together the flour, baking powder, coconut, and salt, then set aside. In a large bowl, cream together the butter and sugar until pale and fluffy. Next, whisk in the lime juice, lime zest, eggs, and vanilla until smooth. If the mixture begins to separate slightly, don't worry, as it will come together once you add the rest of the ingredients.

Alternate the coconut milk with the flour mixture, starting with coconut milk and ending with the flour. You'll need to alternate around three times with each, so each time add a third of the material. This helps to ensure that everything combines properly.

Pour the batter into the loaf tin and bake the cake for 45 to 50 minutes or until a toothpick inserted comes out clean and the top is a beautiful golden brown. If the cake begins to brown too much, you can slide a piece of aluminum foil over the top (after around 30 min of baking) and continue baking the cake with the foil.

Let the cake cool for around 10 minutes, then remove it from the loaf tin and let it cool completely on a wire rack.

To make the glaze, combine the lime juice and confectioners' sugar until it has a smooth, runny consistency, adding a touch more lime juice if necessary.

To serve the cake, remove it from the parchment paper and place on your serving plate. Drizzle with the glaze, letting it drip down the sides. Then sprinkle the cake with lime zest and desiccated coconut. You can enjoy this cake warm, or at room temperature.

Storing: The cake lasts for up to a week if stored properly, but, like all cakes, is best served immediately.

Orange, Olive Oil, and Poppyseed Cake with Macerated Strawberries

Prep time: 25 min

Cook time: 1 hour

Makes: 8–10 servings

For the cake:

2 tablespoons orange zest

325 g / 11.5 oz (1½ cups) granulated sugar

300 g / 10.6 oz (2 cups) all-purpose flour

35 g / 1.2 oz (¼ cup) poppy seeds

1½ teaspoons salt

1 teaspoon baking powder

½ teaspoon baking soda

250 mL / 8.5 fl oz (1 cup) olive oil

250 mL / 8.5 fl oz (1 cup) milk

125 mL / 4.2 fl oz (½ cup) fresh orange juice

3 large eggs

For the macerated strawberries:

425 g / 15 oz (3 cups) strawberries, quartered

2 tablespoons balsamic vinegar

1–2 tablespoons granulated sugar

1 tablespoon orange juice (juice of half an orange)

Whipped cream or crème fraiche for serving (optional)

Olive oil has a miraculous effect on food, adding a richness, and bringing out hidden flavors. In this recipe, olive oil is combined with orange and poppyseeds, bringing you an aromatic cake with a slightly squidgy interior that melts in your mouth. Olive oil is richer than butter and has a more pronounced flavor. The combination of orange and olive oil gives this cake a Mediterranean vibe, perfect for spring (but really, any time of year). I like to pair this cake with macerated strawberries: the sweet, syrupy fruit adds a fresh contrast to the subtle flavors of the cake, a welcome and delicious addition.

Preheat the oven to 180°C or 350°F, and grease a 22-to-24-cm (9-inch) cake tin with oil or butter. Then line the bottom of the tin with parchment paper and set aside. In a large bowl, whisk together the orange zest and granulated sugar. Stir in the flour, poppyseeds, salt, baking powder, and baking soda.

In another bowl, combine the olive oil, milk, orange juice, and eggs. Don't worry if the mixture separates slightly. Make a well in the center of the dry ingredients, and pour in the wet ingredients. Whisk together just until everything is well-incorporated, scraping down the sides of the bowl as necessary. Pour the batter into the prepared cake tin, and bake for an hour, or until the top turns golden and a toothpick inserted comes out clean, with a few damp crumbs. Let the cake cool completely.

To loosen the cake, run a knife around the edges and remove from the cake tin. Gently remove the cake and peel off the parchment, then place on a plate.

While the cake is baking, prepare the strawberries by combining them with the balsamic vinegar (trust me on this one!), sugar, and orange juice in a bowl. Stir together, then cover the bowl and keep the strawberries at room temperature for around 20 minutes, or slightly longer in the refrigerator, until they release some of their juices. Serve the strawberries immediately.

Storing: While the strawberries last up to a day, the cake can last up to a week if stored properly, but like any cake, it is best enjoyed fresh.

The Best Carrot Cake

Prep time: 30 min

Cook time: 45–60 min

Makes: 12–16 pieces

For the cake:

360 g / 12.7 oz (2 ⅔ cups) all-purpose flour

1½ teaspoons baking powder

1½ teaspoons baking soda

1 teaspoon salt

1½ teaspoons cinnamon

1 teaspoon nutmeg

½ teaspoon allspice

500 g / 17.6 oz (4 cups) carrot, shredded—roughly 6–8 carrots

60 mL / 2 fl oz (¼ cup) lemon juice

400 g / 14.1 oz (2 cups) granulated sugar

300 mL / 10.1 fl oz (1¼ cup) flavorless oil (such as canola or vegetable)

1½ teaspoons vanilla extract

4 large eggs

130 g / 4.6 oz (1 heaping cup) unsalted walnuts or pecans, chopped (you can increase the quantity to 1½ cups if you like)*

For the cream cheese frosting:

60 g / 2.1 oz (¼ cup) unsalted butter, softened

125 g / 4.4 oz cream cheese at room temperature

1 teaspoon vanilla extract

1 tablespoon freshly squeezed lemon juice

2 cups (250 g / 8.8 oz) confectioners' sugar

Cinnamon for dusting (optional)

50 g / 1.8 oz (½ cup) unsalted walnuts, chopped, to garnish (optional)

This is the first carrot cake recipe I ever made, and the only carrot cake recipe I will ever make. It's moist, full of warm flavors, and incredibly tender. The nuts bring a nice bite, and the cream cheese frosting adds a lush, zingy note. My sister's friend Danika shared the recipe years ago, when they were still in high school. The original version was carefully created by Danika's father Lee, who tested and retested it until it was perfect. Perfectly soft, perfectly spiced, just the right amount of sugar: you won't find a better cake out there. I'm truly grateful to Danika and Lee for sharing it with me, and for letting me share it with you.

To make the cake, preheat the oven to 180°C or 350°F, grease a 20x30-cm (approx. 9x13-inch) pan with butter and dust with flour. In a small bowl, stir together the dry ingredients (flour, baking powder, baking soda, salt, cinnamon, nutmeg, and allspice) and set aside.

In another bowl, toss the carrots with the lemon juice and set aside. In a large bowl, blend the sugar, oil, vanilla, and eggs until smooth. Add the flour mixture, stirring just to combine. Fold in the carrot mixture and nuts. The nuts are optional, but I highly recommend adding them! You can also add in chocolate chips or raisins if you like.

Pour the mixture into the prepared pan and bake for 45–60 minutes (if baking multiple layers, the baking time will need to be adjusted accordingly), or until a toothpick inserted comes out clean. Cool completely before frosting.

To make the frosting, blend together the butter, cream cheese, vanilla, and lemon juice.

Gradually add in the confectioners' sugar and beat until smooth. The frosting should hold a soft peak when you lift up the whisk/beater. Note that it is thinner than regular buttercream, so it is not the best frosting for piping, but it tastes glorious with this cake.

You can then garnish the cake with some cinnamon and chopped nuts, but this is totally optional.

Storing: This cake lasts over a week if tightly wrapped, sealed, and stored in the fridge. Once frosted, store for up to five days in the fridge.

Note: You can also add in a handful of chocolate chips, raisins, or desiccated coconut.

Mazurek-Inspired Millionaire's Shortbread

Prep time: 1 hour

Cook time: 40–45 min in total

Serves: 20–25 bars or small squares

For the base:

150 g / 5.3 oz (¾ cup) unsalted butter, softened at room temperature

50 g / 1.8 oz (¼ cup) dark brown sugar, packed

½ teaspoon vanilla extract

½ teaspoon salt

200 g / 7.1 oz (1½ cups) all-purpose flour

For the caramel*

75 g / 2.6 oz (6 tablespoons) unsalted butter

75 g / 2.6 oz (6 tablespoons) dark brown sugar, packed

1 can (397 g / 14 oz / 1¼ cup) sweetened condensed milk

1 teaspoon vanilla extract

1 teaspoon salt

For the topping:

200 g / 7.1 oz dark chocolate, at least 50 percent cacao solids (I use 75 percent)

175 mL / 5.9 fl oz (¾ cup) heavy whipping cream

Flaked almonds, chopped nuts, dried fruit, or extra dulce de leche to decorate

This recipe is inspired by *Mazurek*, a sweet, flat Polish Easter cake made of shortcrust pastry, topped with jam, or maybe some chocolate, dulce de leche caramel or *"kajmak,"* nuts, and dried fruit. This version is reminiscent of a chocolate caramel *Mazurek (Mazurek Kajmakowy-Czedoladowo)*, available at one of my favorite cafes in Warsaw during the spring. It is similar to a millionaire's shortbread, comprising a layer of buttery brown sugar cookie, dulce de leche caramel *(kajmak)*, and a silky chocolate ganache. I normally make this recipe in a square tin and finish it with flaked almonds, nuts, or dried fruit and slice into squares, a hybrid between millionaire's shortbread and *Mazurek*. For a more traditional *Mazurek*-like appearance, you can serve in its full form: make it in a larger tin or form the shortbread into a circular shape (or an egg for Easter!), creating a thicker outer ridge as the border. Then fill with the caramel, top with ganache, and decorate with nuts and dried fruit as you like.

To begin, preheat the oven to 180°C or 350°F, grease a baking tin with butter and line it with parchment paper. I use a 22-cm (9-inch) square tin, but a slightly larger one will also work fine for thinner layers. You can also do this in a circular tin if you wish to serve it whole.

Cream together the butter, brown sugar, vanilla, and salt until smooth. Add in the flour and mix until the ingredients merge into a thick, sand-colored mass. Press the mixture evenly into the prepared tin (or shape as you like), then prick generously with a fork. Bake the crust for 20–25 minutes or until the edges turn a nice golden brown.

Let the crust cool. In the meantime, prepare the caramel filling if you're making it.

In a medium-sized non-stick saucepan over medium heat, combine the butter, sugar, and sweetened condensed milk. Continuously stir the ingredients together using a rubber spatula, until the sugar and butter have completely melted and blended into the condensed milk. Let the mixture come to a boil, then reduce the heat to low and let the mixture thicken, stirring constantly. It will take around 5 minutes, and when thickened, you should be able to see traces of the spatula in the mixture, and if you run your finger through the back of the spatula, the caramel should stay in place (you should be able to see the line). When you notice the mixture is thick, turn off the heat and stir in the vanilla and salt. Next, pour the caramel over the crust, and let it cool completely. You can pop the tray into the freezer to speed up the process, but it should take about 30 min to an hour. When the caramel is set, you can spread the chocolate ganache on top.

To make the ganache, break or chop the chocolate into small pieces and place in a heatproof bowl. Next, bring the heavy whipping cream to a boil, either in the microwave for about a minute and a half, or in a saucepan over the stovetop. Pour the heavy whipping cream over the chocolate, and let the mixture sit for around 30 seconds. Stir the ingredients together until blended. In the beginning, the mixture will look slightly separated, but keep stirring, it will come together beautifully. When the ganache is silky smooth, spread it atop the caramel. Sprinkle it with flaked almonds or any nuts or dried fruit of your choice.

Chill the Mazurek again until the chocolate layer is firmer, for around an hour. You can also pipe on small rosettes of extra dulce de leche if you have it (this is how they do it in the café I like).

Serve whole, as is done with a Mazurek, or cut into squares, as is done with a Millionaire's Shortbread. I like this dessert best when it is cold and the layers are rather firm.

It is quite rich (perhaps the title "Millionaire's Shortbread" is fitting)—be sure to cut it into small servings.

Storing: This dessert lasts about a week if sealed properly.

Note: You can replace the homemade caramel with store-bought dulce de leche or caramel. You'll need around 400 g / 14.1 oz or 1¼ cups.

May

May reminds me of our garden at home in Poland, which begins to come alive around this time of year. It is our favorite part of the house. On good days, the sun is out and the sky is a sea of blue. Flowers are beginning to bloom. The days grow longer and the sunsets are golden. Sometimes my dad will turn on the grill. Sometimes we pull out the Frisbees and badminton rackets, delaying dinner to remain outside. Sometimes my mom walks barefoot on the grass, soaking it in. It is peaceful, a sanctuary.

It is in this spirit that I share with you recipes that mark the end of spring and beginning of summer, starting with the Mango Trifle, a bold, celebratory creation to welcome the warm weather. Mangoes are likely my favorite fruit: the small, sunset-colored Alphonsos take me back to India. Although the recipe calls for mangoes, if you can't find them in your part of the world, any other fruit will work for this recipe. Next is an easy homemade ice cream requiring only two key ingredients, the rest being up to your imagination! My preferred version is a Raspberry and Stracciatella (pictured). Another easy and healthier recipe follows: my favorite version of a Coffee Shake. I make this smoothie nearly every day that I'm home during the summer because 1) caffeine and 2) keeps you cool and 3) it's delicious! Last is my No-Bake Fruit Tart, an easy, elegant way to serve up whatever fruit you have on hand without turning on the oven. Summer, we are ready for you.

Regal Mango Trifle

Prep time: 1 hour
Cook time: 10–15 min
Makes: 8–10 servings

For the custard:

4 large egg yolks*
75 g / 2.6 oz (6 tablespoons) granulated sugar
2 tablespoons cornstarch
A pinch of salt
375 mL / 12.7 fl oz (1½ cups) whole milk
1 tablespoon orange zest, or the zest of 1 large orange (optional)
1 tablespoon unsalted butter
1 teaspoon vanilla extract

For the trifle layers:

The flesh of 2 large, ripe mangoes
75 mL / 2.5 fl oz (6 tablespoons) orange or mango juice
300 mL / 10.1 fl oz (1¼ cup) heavy whipping cream, 35–36 percent fat solids
1 tablespoon granulated sugar
1 teaspoon vanilla extract
250 g / 8.8 oz (4 cups, cubed) vanilla pound cake (babka) store-bought or homemade—see Victoria sponge on p. 113 to make your own; one layer of the cake is enough
1 large, ripe mango, sliced, to decorate
Passionfruit pulp (the pulp of 3–4 fresh passionfruit) to decorate

In India, we refer to the mango as the king of all fruit: they can be eaten by the dozen, plain, in a beverage, a curry, a pickled item, a dessert, or a dried snack: the possibilities are endless. It is probably the most popular natural confection in the country and exists in over forty varieties. Mangoes are also my favorite fruit: I love the sunset-orange ones, Kesar or Alphonso, that are juicy, ripe, and sweet. If any of our relatives visit us in Poland from India during peak mango season, we always request a box of mangoes. Mangoes are a luxury to me, and I devour them plain and savor the fruit bite by bite. But when you are blessed with a surplus of the fruit, this recipe is a glorious way to make use of them. Elegantly arranged layers of mango, custard, cream, and cake make for an impressive centerpiece, fit for festive summer gatherings, or if you're like me, Christmas dinner (we get nice mangoes in Poland around December). Either way, you won't be able to get enough. And should you wish to replace the mangoes, use any fruit you like. The Roasted Rhubarb (p. 129) is a nice alternative, as are berries, bananas, peaches—you name it.

To make the custard, begin by whisking together the egg yolks, sugar, cornstarch, and salt until thick and smooth. Then set aside. In the meantime, heat the milk (and orange zest if using) in a small saucepan until it starts to steam, and bubbles appear on the edges (not boiling, but scalding). At this point, very (very!) slowly pour the milk into the egg mixture to temper it. Start with a few tablespoons, then pour in all the milk in a thin, steady stream. Be careful, though! Don't add the milk all at once, as you might end up with scrambled eggs. Going slowly is key.

Pour the egg mixture back into the saucepan, and place over low heat, stirring constantly.

Bring the mixture to a boil until it is thick. It may take a few minutes to boil (3–5 min) but once it does, it will thicken quite quickly: you should be able to see the whisk's path in the mixture, and if you dip a spatula in and run your finger across it, the line in the custard should stay in place.

At this point, turn the heat off, and place a fine-mesh sieve over a medium-sized bowl. Pour the custard through the sieve into the bowl and whisk in the butter and vanilla.

Strain it using a fine-mesh sieve into a bowl and add the butter and vanilla, stirring gently till the butter has melted. Cover the surface of the custard with a piece of cling wrap to prevent a skin from forming and let it cool to room temperature. Then chill the custard in the fridge for several hours or until cold.

You can enjoy the custard with various pies, use it as a filling for tarts, or, of course, in this trifle. It will last just about 5 days in the fridge.

To assemble the trifle, cut each mango in three parts lengthwise. You should end up with two halves and one middle portion containing the seeds. Scoop the flesh out of the mango. I like to do this by scoring the halves in a criss-cross pattern till it barely touches the bottom, then using a spoon to scoop it out. For the seed, just peel the skin and use a knife to scrape the flesh. Place the mango in a small bowl and pour the orange or mango juice over it. Let it sit, covered, in the fridge, while you prepare the rest of the ingredients.

Whip the cream with the sugar and vanilla until you get a nice, stiff peak (if you lift the beaters or whisk, the peak should hold its shape). This will take 5 to 10 min, but don't overbeat, as that will cause the cream to curdle. It's better to have a softer peak than curdled cream!

Take the custard out of the fridge and fold it into about a third of the freshly whipped cream, reserving the rest of the cream for the trifle. Next, cut the pound cake into 2-to-3-cm cubes (1 to 1.5 inches).

To make this trifle, you'll need a large dish. I use a 22-cm (9-inch) trifle dish, but a glass bowl will work fine too. Of course, any dish would work, but it's nice to see the layers.

Evenly scatter the pound cake cubes on the bottom of the dish. Pour the mango mixture and all the fruit over the top of the pound cake as evenly as possible. Next, spread the custard mixture atop the fruit and cake. Add the remaining ⅔ of whipped cream, covering to coat the custard completely. To finish the trifle, scatter the extra sliced mango on top for garnish, and drizzle a bit of passionfruit pulp for a bolder finish.

Storing: You can serve the trifle immediately, or chill for several hours before serving. Whipped cream and fruit are best enjoyed fresh, so I would prepare this at most several hours in advance.

Notes:

- For a quicker, eggless version, you can skip making the vanilla custard from scratch and use store-bought vanilla pudding mix or custard powder. Follow the instructions on the package.

- To make this recipe eggless, I recommend using instant pudding mix or custard powder, I don't recommend replacing egg yolks. However, I have tried vanilla pudding without eggs. You'll need to increase the milk to 625 mL / 21.1 fl oz (2½ cups) and amp up the amount of cornstarch to 3 tablespoons. It may not be quite as rich, but if you add a good amount of vanilla, the pudding will still work nicely in a trifle.

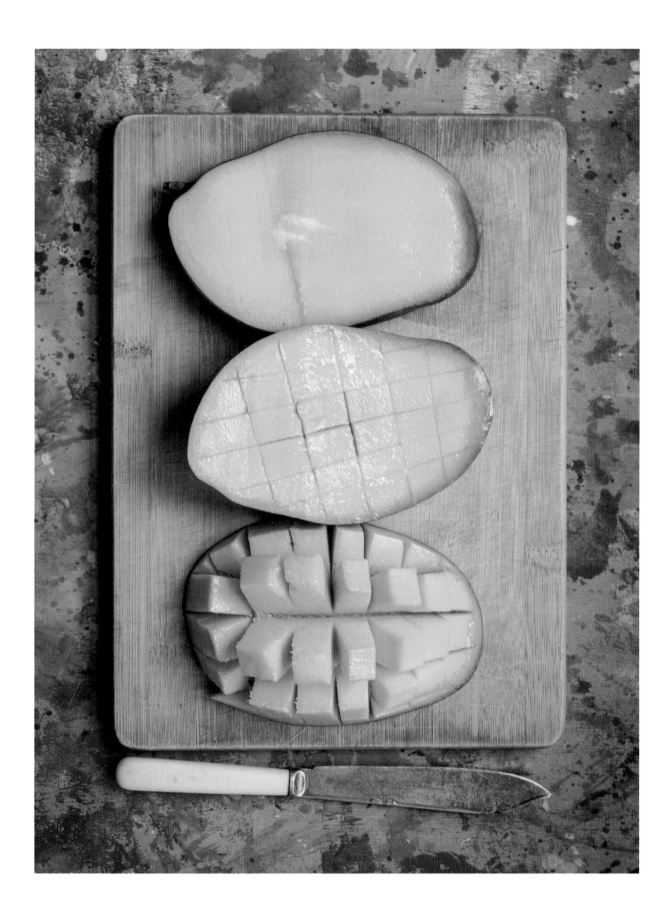

No-Churn Stracciatella and Raspberry Ice Cream

Prep time: 10 minutes

Cook time: None!

Makes: 4 cups (1 liter) of ice cream

Ingredients

500 mL / 16.9 fl oz (2 cups) heavy whipping cream, chilled

2 teaspoons vanilla extract

325 g / 11.5 oz (1 cup) sweetened condensed milk

100 g / 3.5 oz (⅔ cup) dark chocolate, grated or finely chopped

150 g / 5.3 oz (1 heaping cup) frozen raspberries, roughly broken/chopped

A few summers ago, no-churn ice cream went viral on the internet. Although no-machine ice cream recipes have always been available, none compare to this one: creamy, smooth, devoid of ice crystals, and extremely quick to throw together. The result is nearly comparable to one you'd expect from an ice cream machine, minus all the fuss. Like any ice cream recipe, this one starts with a three-ingredient base that can be tweaked and twisted—here's where you can really get creative with flavors. I've given a couple ideas below, but really, the possibilities are endless.

First, beat the cream and vanilla extract until it begins to form soft peaks that hold their shape. Pour in the sweetened condensed milk and continue to beat the mixture until it forms soft peaks once more—the mixture should be thick, and if you run your finger through, it should hold its shape. It doesn't need to be stiff or firm, though. Fold in the dark chocolate and frozen raspberries. (For other varieties, see below.) Pour the mixture into a loaf tin and cover it with cling film, or into a Tupperware container with a lid. Freeze the mixture for at least 2 hours or until solid.

Storing: The ice cream lasts for several months, if frozen properly.

Variations

Cookies and Crème:
150 g / 5.3 oz (1½ cup) of your favorite cookie, crushed
Fold into the ice cream base before freezing.

Dulce de leche:
Replace the sweetened condensed milk with a can of dulce de leche. Add ½ teaspoon salt to the ice cream base.

Bourbon Vanilla:
30 mL / 1 fl oz (2 tablespoons) bourbon
1 vanilla bean, split lengthwise, seeds scraped out
Fold into the ice cream base before freezing.

Chocolate:
100 g / 3.5 oz dark chocolate
Add 125 mL / 4.2 fl oz (½ cup) of the ice cream base to the chocolate, and melt together over a double boiler or in the microwave until smooth. Let it cool to room temperature, then stir into the ice cream base.

Eton Mess:
Fold in a handful of meringue cookies, crushed, and a handful of frozen raspberries or strawberries, chopped or broken. I like to let the frozen fruit sit for around 5 minutes and chop it finely. You can also throw the fruit in a food processor and blitz, then swirl into the mix.

Coffee Shake

Prep time: 2 min

Cook time: None!

Makes: 1 tall glass, or 2 small

Ingredients

250 mL / 8.5 fl oz (1 cup) milk of your choice (I use 2 percent)*

1 teaspoon instant espresso powder (more if needed)*

1 ripe banana, sliced and frozen (150 g / 5.3 oz / around ¾–1 cup sliced)*

1 date, pitted (10 g / 0.4 oz) or 1 tablespoon honey (for sweetness)

This is my go-to afternoon treat during the summer: I make it daily when spending summers at home, divided into two small glasses, one for my mom and one for me. It's a healthier version of a Frappuccino: rich, creamy, and infused with caffeine to help with that afternoon slump. This drink is also deliciously refreshing, perfect for those hot summer days.

Combine the milk, espresso powder, sliced banana, and date or honey in a blender, and blitz till smooth. Because of the frozen banana and dates, it might take a few minutes, as you want everything to be nice and creamy. I find this to be the perfect consistency; it's thick, yet drinkable.

For a thinner consistency, add more milk, and for something more like an ice cream, you can reduce the milk by half.

Serve immediately.

Notes:

♦ You can use any milk you like; non-dairy milk works fine too!

♦ You can increase the coffee in this recipe by adding 2 teaspoons instead of 1 for a more pronounced flavor

♦ I like to freeze bananas in bulk by storing them in a Ziploc bag and freezing, then taking them out of the freezer when I need to and slicing them with a sharp knife. You can also slice them, place the slices apart on a parchment-lined tray, then freeze and transfer to Ziploc bags.

Fabulously Easy No-Bake Fruit Tart

Prep time: 30 min
Cook time: 2–5 min
Makes: 8 servings

For the base:
200 g / 7.1 oz plain cookies (such as tea biscuits, graham crackers, or digestive biscuits) (2 cups of cookie crumbs)
125 g / 4.4 oz (heaping ½ cup) unsalted butter, melted

For the filling:
200 g / 7.1 oz (around 1⅓ cups) white chocolate, roughly chopped
250 g / 8.8 oz (around 1 cup) mascarpone cheese
250 mL / 8.5 fl oz (1 cup) heavy whipping cream, cold
1 teaspoon vanilla extract

Topping:
Fresh fruit, such as mangoes, strawberries, kiwis, blueberries, etc.

As summer makes its debut, so do strawberries, cherries, blueberries, blackberries, peaches, and mangoes, adding bold hues to grocery aisles and delicious, fresh flavors to your baking. Colorful fruit, either neatly arranged or scattered, is art in edible form. Complemented by a decadent white chocolate mascarpone mousse-like filling, and a crisp cookie base, this easily customizable recipe works well with virtually any kind of fruit.

To make the base, pulse the cookies in a food processor until you are left with a smooth rubble. If you don't have a food processor, you can place the cookies in a Ziploc bag and whack them with a rolling pin until the cookies are completely crushed. Tip the cookie crumbs into a bowl, and pour in the melted butter. Mix the ingredients together until you have something that resembles damp sand. Next, press the mixture into a tart tin (with a removable base around 22cm or 9 inches in diameter) and up the sides, using your fingertips and the back of a spoon. If you don't have a tart tin, you can use any sort of presentable dish around the same size, or simply press the cookies into a cake tin and slightly up the sides to create a crater of sorts. Place the crust in the fridge to chill while you prepare the filling.

For the filling, begin by melting the white chocolate. You can do this in the microwave, stirring every 30 seconds, until the chocolate is smooth. You can also do this step on the stovetop over very low heat, stirring slowly but constantly, or over a double boiler (perhaps the safest method). Chocolate can burn quickly (you'll know when it starts to clump up and turn grainy), so it's important to keep a close eye on it while it is melting. When the chocolate is liquified and smooth, turn off the heat and let it cool to room temperature.

While the chocolate is cooling, beat together the mascarpone cheese and heavy whipping cream, until you're left with soft peaks. If you lift your whisk or beaters from the bowl, the peak should hold. I do this step by hand (it's a good workout), but you can use an electric mixer to speed up the process. Slowly stir in the melted chocolate and the vanilla, scraping the bottom and the sides of the bowl, just until you're left with a thick, silky smooth mass.

Pour the filling into the tart tin. Try to add as much as you can. If some is still left, it's so good by itself you could eat it by the spoonful or serve it with fruit as its own dessert. Let the tart chill in the fridge for several hours, then top with sliced fruit just before serving.

Storing: Because this recipe contains fresh cream and fruit, it should really be eaten the day it is made. The tart with the filling can be made a few hours in advance, but once you top it with the fruit, it should be served as soon as possible.

June

June officially marks the start of summer, partly because school finishes for the year, and partly because June 21 is the longest day of the summer. Since leaving home for university, it is during the summer holiday that I return home. During the day, my family and I each do our own thing. For me, that means endless streams of sugar, as I take my holiday to prepare much of the content for my blog. But in the evening, my family gathers in the garden for a drink before dinner, taking advantage of the evening light.

It is rare for all four of us to be on the same continent, let alone the same country, at a given moment. Yet summer draws us home, and I cherish the moments we share together. To mark the official beginning of summer, I present you with an assortment of recipes that can be customized as per your fruit preference, using whatever is in season.

First up is my Pineapple Upside-Down Cake recipe, a soft vanilla cake studded with bright yellow fruit, beautiful without additional embellishments. Its vibrant color is fitting for the occasion. In the spirit of the no-bake theme is my Eton Mess recipe, a pudding composed of meringue, cream, and fruit. It is another wonder that can be assembled in minutes. Wimbledon, the popular tennis tournament, takes place annually in June, and Eton Mess is a tradition for the occasion—now you can prepare it at home. In case you prefer not to turn on your oven during the hotter months, I have you covered with my favorite Better than Anything Biscuit Cake, a magical creation using whatever fruit you fancy. Last, but not least, is my Victoria Sponge Cake recipe, a celebratory cake, in honor of my sister.

Pineapple Upside-Down Cake

Prep time: 25 min

Cook time: 25–30 min

Serves: 8–10

Topping:

60 g / 2.1 oz (¼ cup) unsalted butter, melted

100 g / 3.5 oz (½ cup) brown sugar

Around ¾ of a fresh pineapple (you can also use around 9–12 canned slices)

Cake:

75 g / 2.6 oz (⅓ cup) unsalted butter, softened

130 g / 4.6 oz (⅔ cup) granulated sugar

1 large egg

½ teaspoon vanilla extract

1½ teaspoons baking powder

½ teaspoon salt

175 mL / 5.9 fl oz (¾ cup) buttermilk

160 g / 5.6 oz (1⅓ cups) all-purpose flour

One of the most stunning culinary gems is pineapple, encased in a criss-cross yellow-green coating, hatted with leaves that resemble a fountain. If you're looking for a fuss-free recipe designed to impress, this one is it: a single layer, no icing, no exotic ingredients (besides the pineapple). It is a basic vanilla cake with a caramelized layer of fruit. If fresh pineapple is unavailable, canned pineapple works just fine, as do strawberries, cherries, apricots, peaches, pears, and apples.

First, preheat the oven to 180°C or 350°F and grease a 23-cm (9-inch) dish with butter. To make the topping, combine melted butter and brown sugar directly in the prepared cake pan. You should be left with a thick, caramel-colored mixture. Spread the mixture as evenly as possible to cover the bottom of the cake pan, then set aside while you prepare the pineapple.

To cut the pineapple, chop off the top and bottom, then trim off the skin. I like to slice the pineapple horizontally (to get disks), then cut each disk into cubes, leaving out the center part. You could also use a cookie cutter to cut out the center part, resulting in rings of pineapple instead of pieces. Arrange the pineapple pieces over the brown sugar mixture. I also like to add pineapple pieces up the sides of the cake pan. When you're happy with the arrangement of pineapple pieces, set the cake pan aside while you prepare the vanilla cake batter.

To make the cake, cream together the butter and sugar until light and fluffy. Next, whisk in the egg and vanilla. Add in the baking soda and salt, and then pour in the buttermilk. The mixture may separate at this point, but it will come together once you add the flour. Toss in the flour, stirring slowly, just until combined. Once the batter comes together, spread it atop the pineapple and brown sugar mixture. Bake the cake for 25 to 30 min or until a toothpick inserted comes out clean and the top is a nice golden brown. Let the cake cool for several minutes, then gently loosen it with a butter knife.

To release the cake, work quickly, as the sugar-butter mixture will begin to solidify with cooling, making it more difficult to release the cake from the pan. Place a plate on top of the cake dish, making sure that your hands are well protected. In one swift motion, flip the cake over, tapping on the bottom of the cake pan to release it. Let it sit like this for several minutes, then gently pull up the cake tin. It is fine if some of the pineapple pieces stick to the cake tin; just remove them from the pan and arrange them on the top of the cake. This cake is best served warm.

Storing: Store the cake in the refrigerator, it will last for up to a week.

Eton Mess

Prep time: 15 minutes

Cook time: None (if the meringue is already ready!)

Serves: 3-4

Ingredients

200 g / 7.1 oz (1½ cups) fresh raspberries or strawberries (sliced)*

½ tablespoon balsamic vinegar

200 mL / 6.8 fl oz heavy whipping cream (35-36 percent), chilled*

½ tablespoon granulated sugar

1 teaspoon vanilla extract

75 g / 2.6 oz (about 2 cups) plain meringues, roughly crumbled (like broken cookies)

More raspberries and meringue for topping

Born at Eton College in England, the Eton Mess was served at the school's annual cricket match. Thankfully, the dessert spread far beyond the boarding school. It is made up of three main ingredients: fruit, cream, and meringue, making it gluten-free, no-bake, and perfect for lazy summer days. Traditionally, this recipe is made with strawberries, but I quite like it with raspberries as well. The addition of balsamic vinegar to the raspberries transforms the fruit into a lush, syrupy heap that radiates through the snowy meringue and cream. You can use store-bought meringues to make this dessert, but you can also make your own (see the pavlova on p. 177)

In a small bowl, combine the raspberries or strawberries and the balsamic vinegar. If using raspberries, gently mash them only slightly. This will help release some of the juices. Set aside.

Next, whip the cold heavy whipping cream with the sugar and vanilla until the cream forms peaks (it should take a few minutes). If you lift the beaters or whisk from the bowl, it should hold its shape. Don't overbeat, as the mixture will begin to separate and if you overmix, you might end up with butter! Gently fold in the crushed meringue. Lastly, fold in the fruit. Do this gently, so that your result is more of a marbled mixture. You can also layer the fruit and the cream when serving (see next step).

Prepare four dessert glasses and divide the mixture between each. You can also serve the pudding in a larger dish. If you choose to layer the cream and fruit, alternate the cream mixture with the berries in dollops. Top with additional meringue and fruit to finish. Serve immediately.

Storing: This dessert is best eaten right away, as the longer you wait, the less crisp the meringues will be, and since you use fresh cream and fruit, it really tastes best soon after being prepared.

Notes:

- You can use different fruit for this recipe (just omit the balsamic vinegar). You can also use frozen berries, thawed and slightly drained.

- The cream should be cold, as should (ideally) the bowl and whisk. This helps the cream whip. If it's too hot, the cream might separate and will probably not whip as easily.

Better than Anything Biscuit Cake

Prep time: 20 min
Cook time: 2–3 min
Serves: 6–8

For the biscuit cake:

500 mL / 16.9 fl oz (2 cups) cold heavy whipping cream (35–36 percent fat solids)

1 can (approx. 390 g / 13.8 oz / 1¼ cups) sweetened condensed milk

2 teaspoons vanilla extract

250 g / 8.8 oz Marie biscuits or any plain, light cookie (around 60; I use 12–16 per layer)*

250 mL / 8.5 fl oz (1 cup) strong, black coffee, cooled (you can also dissolve 2 teaspoons instant espresso powder in 1 cup hot water, then cool)*

For the topping:

125 g / 4.4 oz (½ cup) chocolate, at least 50 percent cacao solids

125 mL / 4.2 fl oz (½ cup) heavy whipping cream

Fresh strawberries (I use 200 g / 7.1 oz, or around 2 heaping cups), sliced

This dessert is sort of a cheat tiramisu and has the best qualities of both a pudding and a cake. The layers alternate between cookies dipped in coffee, which miraculously turn into cake layers, and what I like to call a vanilla mousse (think vanilla ice cream, but not frozen). The rich chocolate ganache and strawberries take it to the next level, though feel free to use bananas or other berries in place of the strawberries. In economic terms, this dessert gives maximum returns: it requires minimal effort, zero ovens, and yields the highest amount of satisfaction. No one will be able to tell how easy it is to make, considering its majestic appearance (luscious strawberries layered upon a bed of chocolate do the trick) and fusion of "cake" with creamy goodness. It is a great make-ahead dessert, perfect for summer, but really for any time of year.

Combine the chilled heavy whipping cream and sweetened condensed milk in a large bowl, and whip to a soft peak. You'll be able to see clear streaks of the whisk or beater in the mixture, and when you lift it, the peak should hold its shape with the top falling over slightly, like soft-serve ice cream. It takes around 10 minutes by hand but will go by faster with an electric whisk. Be careful not to overbeat, as that might cause the mixture to curdle.

Gently stir in the vanilla extract.

Begin by arranging a layer of biscuits on the bottom of your cake tin—you'll need around 12 to 16, but perhaps more depending on the dish you use. Dip each cookie in the cooled coffee and place the biscuits close together to form a bottom layer. If necessary, you can break the cookies into smaller pieces to fill large gaps. I like to use a 22-cm (9-inch) springform cake tin. You can use any dish that is roughly the same size to make this recipe and serve it in the dish itself.

Next, add approximately a third of the cream mixture, and spread it out evenly. Add another layer of the cookies, another layer of cream, another layer of cookies, and another layer of cream, ending with a layer of cookies. You should have four cookie layers in total. Cover with cling wrap and place in the refrigerator overnight or for 6 to 8 hours minimum. This will allow the cookies to soften and become more "cakey," and will allow the flavors to merge slightly.

To make the ganache, break the chocolate and place in a small heatproof bowl. Bring the heavy whipping cream to a boil, either in a small saucepan over medium heat or in the microwave, heating for about a minute to a minute and a half. Pour the cream over the chocolate and let the mixture sit for around 30 seconds. Stir until smooth and silky, then let it cool to room temperature.

If you are using a springform cake tin, loosen the cake by running a knife around the edges, then gently remove it from the tin. Place the cake on a nice plate or cake stand. Pour the cooled ganache atop the biscuit cake and spread it slightly so that it drips down the sides. Chill the cake until you are ready to serve or serve immediately. Right before serving, top the cake with the fresh strawberries.

Storing: This dessert is best enjoyed after 24 hours if making without the strawberries but can be frozen for several weeks if wrapped in plastic wrap and sealed properly. Thaw and store in the refrigerator overnight before serving. Top with the fruit immediately before serving.

Notes:

- You can use Marie biscuits or can replace them with tea biscuits, any other plain cookie, or cookie that you like, such as chocolate cookies, gingersnap cookies—you name it.

- You can really play around with this recipe: for a chocolate version, infuse the cream with 75 to 100 g / 2.6 to 3.5 oz of melted and cooled bittersweet chocolate. For an intense coffee version, add 2 teaspoons of instant espresso powder to the cream. You can also add fresh fruit to the layers. For more of a banana pudding, add banana slices, or berries, such as strawberries and raspberries. Mangoes and kiwis also work well. This recipe goes with a variety of fruit, and all kinds of biscuits, so feel free to play around!

Victoria Sponge Cake

Prep time: 45 min
Cook time: 20–25 min
Makes: 8–10 servings

For the cake:
225 g / 7.9 oz (1½ cups) all-
   purpose flour
2 teaspoon baking powder
½ teaspoon salt
225 g / 7.9 oz (1 cup) unsalted butter,
   softened at room temperature
225 g / 7.9 oz (1 cup) granulated sugar
1 tablespoon lemon zest (the zest of
   one lemon)
2 teaspoons vanilla extract
4 large eggs
2 tablespoons milk

For the filling:
175 mL / 5.9 fl oz (¾ cup) heavy
   whipping cream (35–36 percent
   fat solids)
1 tablespoon granulated sugar
1 teaspoon vanilla extract
175 g / 6.2 oz (½ cup) jam (I like to use
   strawberry or raspberry)
Extra fruit and jam for topping
Confectioners' sugar for dusting

When I asked one of my friends at university what his favorite cake was, he instantly described a Victoria Sponge Cake; two layers of vanilla cake sandwiched together with whipped cream and fruity jam. Simple. Delicious. I wanted to include this recipe in the summer section, since it allows you to display the luscious fruit that is in abundance when the weather turns warmer. This cake reminds me of the little basket of cakes that appeared in one of my *Little Red Riding Hood* picture books, the ones that Little Red carries to her grandmother. You can use any variety of jam you like, opt for fresh fruit between the layers, or use a combination of the two. I lean toward the traditional version with jam, but finish the cake off with berries to make it truly spectacular.

Preheat the oven to 180°C or 350°F. Generously butter two 20-cm (or 22-cm, 8 or 9 inches) round cake pans, then line the bottom of each tin with a circle of parchment paper. In a small bowl, whisk together the flour, baking powder, and salt, then set aside. Using an electric mixer makes this easier, but you can also do it using a whisk. Next, in a large bowl, beat together the butter, sugar, and lemon zest until light and fluffy.

Pour in the vanilla, and add the eggs one at a time, beating until smooth. Make sure the eggs are at room temperature, as using cold eggs might curdle the mixture (if this does happen, fear not; it will come together once you add the flour). Then, slowly beat in the flour mixture. The mixture should be thick, smooth, and creamy, almost like a mousse. Lastly, whisk in the milk. This should help loosen the batter slightly, especially considering how thick it is.

Divide the batter evenly between the two cake tins, spreading it out as best as you can.

Bake the cakes for 20 to 25 minutes or until a toothpick inserted comes out clean and the cakes turn a beautiful golden brown. If you lightly press on the surface of the cake, it should spring back. Let the cakes cool for around 15 minutes, then run a knife around the edges to loosen them. Flip the cakes onto a cooling rack (you can line the cooling rack with a tea towel to prevent it from marking the cake), and let them cool completely.

Once cooled, you can prepare the whipped cream. The heavy whipping cream should be cold for this step. Pour the cream into a large bowl, along with the sugar and vanilla.

Beat the cream mixture for several minutes, using a whisk (this will take slightly longer) or electric mixer until you're left with a stiff peak. If you lift your beaters from the cream, the peak should hold its shape, but be careful not to overmix, as this will cause the cream to curdle. Set aside.

To assemble, remove the parchment paper from the bottom of the cake, and place on a plate. I do this top-side down. Cover the layer with the jam, evenly. Next, spread the whipped cream on top. It's okay if the two mix slightly, but try to spread the cream gently to prevent this. Remove the parchment from the second layer, and sandwich the cake layer on top of the cream. I do this bottom-side down. To finish the cake, I like to place a tablespoon or so of the jam in the center and spread it out slightly, then arrange additional berries to cover the jam. You can skip this step if you prefer. Finally, dust the cake with confectioners' sugar before serving. This cake makes a lovely teatime snack, something Little Red Riding Hood's grandmother would surely approve.

Storing: It lasts for about a week if covered properly, but should be served quickly once you top with the cream and fruit, as both are best enjoyed immediately.

Variations

Strawberry Cake:
Instead of jam, fill the cake with whipped cream and sliced strawberries, then top with more cream and strawberries. If I'm feeling extra fancy, I also add a small amount of granulated sugar to the strawberries (like the Eton mess, see p. 107). This helps release some of their juices, which can be swirled into the cream for a stunning finish.

Lemon Cake:
For a lemon sponge cake, replace the jam with lemon curd (see p. 75, where the lemon cookies are), top with a bit of the whipped cream and sprinkle with a touch of lemon zest.

Boston Cream Pie:
Replace the jam and whipped cream with a half-quantity of the vanilla pudding (see p. 39, where the chia seed pudding is), and sandwich the cake layers with the pudding. Top with chocolate ganache (see p. 151, where the courgette cake is).

Mocha Cake:
Omit the lemon zest and add 2 tbsp instant espresso powder to the cake batter. Fill with whipped cream, and top with chocolate ganache (see p. 151, where the courgette cake is).

July

In Europe, it is July when summer is really in full swing. Everyone is on vacation mode, escaping to the mountains or the seaside. July moves slowly, allowing one to take the time to relax and enjoy. I usually spend July at home in Poland, and it is really at this time of year that I get a chance to destress and experience boredom for a change, a feeling that is rare during other months of the year. It is in July that I can read a book for fun, spend hours in the kitchen at a time, or bike for pleasure rather than as a means of transport. It is a refreshing change of pace.

It is on this note that I bring you the collection of recipes for the month, refreshing desserts made with lovely summer produce. The *Kersenflappen*, or Cherry Hand Pies are chic pastries filled with cherries and topped with flaked almonds—a perfect snack or treat to enjoy with family and friends. Next up is my Homemade Granola with Grilled Peaches. Because when else do you have a chance to make your own granola from scratch? After that, I present you with one of my all-time favorites, Berry Delicious Cheesecake Brownies, a celebratory recipe, perfect for picnics and barbeques. The final recipe in this section is my Roasted Rhubarb recipe: a simple, summery way to serve rhubarb that goes great with vanilla ice cream.

Kersenflappen (Cherry Hand Pies)

Prep time: 20 min

Cook time: 20–25 min

Makes: 16 pies

Ingredients

2 tablespoons cornstarch

2 tablespoons water

Juice of 1 lemon (around
2 tablespoons)

500 g / 17.6 oz (3 generous cups) tart
fresh or frozen cherries (thawed),
stemmed and pitted*

½ cup (100 g / 3.5 oz) granulated sugar

Pinch of salt

½ teaspoon vanilla extract

720 g / 25.4 oz ready-made puff pastry
(enough for 16)*, or make your own,
(see p. 147's apple pie recipe)

1 egg + 2 tablespoons water for
the egg wash*

Raw sugar for sprinkling (optional)

Fistful of flaked almonds for topping
(optional)

Confectioners' sugar for dusting

This recipe is inspired by the highly popular *appelflappen* that are readily available across the Netherlands: flakey pastry, dusted with sugar and filled with sweet, syrupy cooked apples. In Dutch supermarkets, you can buy packages of puff pastry containing ten 12-cm squares, almost begging for the pastry to be made—all you need to do is stuff it with the apple, fold it diagonally, and bake. But I wanted to take these a step further, so I replaced the apple with cherries. As my housemate says, these *kersenflappen* or cherry hand pies are more chic, and are piled high with flaked almonds and a light dusting of confectioners' sugar to really make them high-class bakery material. This is a recipe fit for cherries, the rubies of the summer.

Preheat the oven to 200°C or 390°F and line two baking trays with parchment paper.

In a small bowl, combine the cornstarch, water, and lemon juice, stirring until smooth.

In a medium-sized pot or saucepan, combine the cherries, the cornstarch mixture, and the sugar. Place the pot over medium heat and bring the cherries to a boil. The cherries should release their juices, and the mixture will thicken, going from a milky pink to deep red. Stir the mixture constantly to prevent the bottom of the pan from burning. This will take around 5 to 10 min. Once it comes to a boil, let the mixture cook for a minute or so longer until it's nice and thick, resembling the consistency of jam. At this point, turn off the heat, and whisk in the salt and vanilla extract.

Next, let this mixture cool completely. This is an important step which I have skipped before, but I have learned from my errors and advise you to wait. The mixture will have a chance to thicken even further, which prevents it from oozing out of the pastry before and during baking. If the mixture is too hot, the puff pastry will melt further (it is kept together with cold butter, and when the butter melts, the pastry becomes sticky), making it incredibly difficult to work with.

I use squares of pastry, 12 cm (around 5 inches) to a side. If you can't find this, you can cut the pastry yourself, using a knife or pizza cutter, into a similar size. You'll need around 16 squares. Place the squares directly onto your baking sheet, around 2 cm (1 inch) apart.

Brush all around the edges of the square with the egg wash (1 egg beaten with 2 tablespoons water).

Spoon 1½ tablespoons of the mixture, around 5 to 6 cherries, into the center of the square. Next, take a corner of the square and fold it over diagonally. You're essentially making a small "flap" or pocket to encase the cherries. To seal the cherries in, press the corners of the square together using a fork, all around the edges (but not necessarily the main fold, the longest side) until completely sealed. Brush the tops of the hand pies with the egg wash, then make two slits in the center of each triangle. This will help hot air escape and will help the pies keep their shape. Sprinkle the tops with raw sugar if using, and generously with the flaked almonds.

Bake the hand pies for 20 to 25 min or until golden brown. A few extra minutes will guarantee a crisp pastry, but be mindful about the flaked almonds, which cook rather quickly, as you don't want to burn them. I find that 23 minutes is perfect for my oven. If you are not using the almonds, then you can bake these for even longer (around 25 to 28 min) for a crispier hand pie. Let the pies cool for around 8 to 10 minutes, then serve warm, with a dusting of confectioners' sugar.

Storing: The pastry is lovely just baked, but these do last for several days if stored properly in the refrigerator (you can reheat them before serving if you like).

Notes:

- I normally use frozen cherries for this recipe, so I can make them throughout the year.

- Puff pastry is often found in the frozen section of your supermarket. In the Netherlands, it's sold in 12x12-cm squares. You'll need enough for 15 to 16 pies. I find it's easiest to buy it based on the mass. In the US, this would be around 3 sheets. You'll need to thaw the pastry before using, but make sure it's still cold. If the pastry is too warm, then it will be difficult to work with. You can also make your own pastry dough—use the dough recipe from the apple pie on p. 147.

- For an egg-free version, replace the egg and water with heavy whipping cream.

- If you want to make these in advance, I'd recommend freezing the trays with the unbaked pastries, then baking for a few extra minutes once you're ready to serve. The frozen, unbaked pastries last around a month

Homemade Granola with Grilled Peaches

Prep time: 10 min
Cook time: 30–35 min (including granola)
Makes: 8–10 servings; enough to last you a week

For the granola:

200 g / 7.1 oz (1½ cups) rolled oats
150 g / 5.3 oz (around 1 cup) nuts and seeds (I use sunflower seeds, pumpkin seeds, and chopped almonds; chia seeds, flax seeds and pecans are also nice)
Handful of dried fruits such as raisins or cranberries (optional)
1½ teaspoons ground cinnamon
2 tablespoons coconut oil or olive oil
4 tablespoons maple syrup or honey, depending on how sweet you like it
40 g / 1.4 oz (½ cup) desiccated coconut

For the peaches (per serving):

1 peach, cut in half and pitted
1 teaspoon coconut oil (melted) or olive oil

Once you try making granola at home, you'll quickly see that supermarket varieties are no match. Although granola is a breakfast food, it can easily be transformed into a dessert, in the form of a parfait, atop some ice cream (see p. 97), or perhaps even as a crumble. The version I'm providing you with is quite standard, but feel free to throw in any other additions you like—puffed rice, dried fruit, any nuts you like, perhaps even some espresso powder to get you through the morning, cacao nibs—you name it. As an ode to summer, I've coupled the granola with grilled peaches and a dollop of thick yogurt, but it's lovely plain as a snack or with some berries or bananas.

For the granola:

Preheat the oven to 150°C (300°F) and line a baking tray with parchment paper. Combine the oats, dried nuts and seeds, dried fruit if using, and the ground cinnamon. In a small saucepan over low heat, warm the oil and honey or maple syrup, but do not bring it to a boil—you only want everything to melt and infuse. Stir the mixture in with the oats until everything is thoroughly incorporated.

Pour the granola onto the prepared baking tray and spread it out in a single layer. Bake the mixture for 20 to 25 minutes or until slightly golden, crisp, and fragrant. Give the mixture a gentle toss and add in the coconut. Put the tray back into the oven for an additional 10 to 15 minutes or until the coconut has toasted and dried—just be careful not to burn the granola. Let the mixture cool on the tray before spooning it into a jar. Serve the granola with your favorite variety of milk, yogurt, and fruit, or as a dessert.

Storing: The granola will store well for several weeks if sealed properly in an airtight container and can be stored at room temperature.

For the peaches:

Place a grill pan (a non-stick saucepan will also work) on the stove and let it heat up. Brush each side of the peach with the oil and place it core side down onto the grill pan. Cook for 4 to 5 minutes on each side or until the core side has caramelized.

Serve warm with the granola and a dollop of yogurt, ricotta cheese, or whipped cream, depending on what you're in the mood for. Serve the peaches immediately after grilling.

Berry Delicious Cheesecake Brownies

Prep time: 30 min

Cook time: 45–50 min

Serves: 16–20

For the brownie base:

200 g / 7.1 oz (1 cup) dark chocolate

200 g / 7.1 oz (1 cup) unsalted butter

3 large eggs

200 g / 7.1 oz (1 cup) sugar (raw, granulated or brown)

125 g / 4.4 oz (¾ cup) all-purpose flour

½ teaspoon baking powder

½ teaspoon salt

1 teaspoon instant espresso powder

For the cheesecake filling:

500 g / 17.6 oz (just over a pound) cream cheese

100 g / 3.5 oz (½ cup) sugar

2 large eggs

40 g / 1.4 oz (1 package, 2 tablespoons) instant vanilla pudding mix (replace with 2 tablespoons cornstarch and 2 teaspoons vanilla if you don't have the pudding)

125 g / 4.4 oz (½ cup) sour cream or heavy whipping cream (35–36 percent fat solids)

250 g / 8.8 oz (around 1¾ cups) berries (I like blueberries and raspberries), fresh or frozen, no need to thaw

A dessert you'll want to roll out the red carpet for, these cheesecake brownies are rich, decadent, and downright delicious. I've made these for numerous birthdays, parties, and other occasions where I want to impress, with berries, raspberries, cherries, or whatever I am in the mood for. This recipe is inspired by the popular "sernikobrownie" on my favorite Polish food blog, *Kwestia Smaku*, which calls for the addition of vanilla pudding. I've also included this in my recipe, and although I try to stay away from store-bought mixes, I have to give in to this hack. It really enhances the flavor and the texture of the cheesecake layer.

Begin by preheating the oven to 170°C or 340°F, and generously grease a large rectangular pan (around 23x33 cm, 9x13 inches, or roughly that size) with butter and line the base with parchment paper.

To make the base, start by melting the chocolate and butter in a medium-sized saucepan over low heat, until smooth. Turn off the heat and let the mixture cool completely.

Pour the chocolate into a large bowl and whisk in the eggs and sugar (you can also do this step in the same pot that you melted the chocolate in). In a small bowl, combine the flour, baking powder, salt, and instant espresso powder. Add this mixture to the chocolate mixture, scraping down the sides of the bowl to make sure everything is incorporated.

Spoon out about a cup of the mixture and set this aside, and spread the remaining brownie batter on the bottom of the prepared pan.

To make the cheesecake filling, combine the cream cheese, sugar, eggs, and vanilla pudding mix, whisking till smooth. It's best if the ingredients are at room temperature as this makes it much easier to combine, and it also helps prevent the cheesecake from cracking later. Fold in the heavy whipping cream or sour cream, just until incorporated. Gently fold about half of the mixed berries into the cheesecake mixture. If you're using frozen berries, make sure they aren't clumped together, but you don't want to thaw them completely, as that will streak the batter.

Pour the cheesecake mixture over the brownie base, spreading it out as evenly as possible.

Next, use a tablespoon to dollop the reserved brownie batter on top. Using a knife, swirl the dolloped brownie batter into the cheesecake mixture. Sprinkle the remaining berries on top as evenly as possible.

Bake the cheesecake brownies for 40 to 45 minutes. Baking the cheesecake in a pan with less surface area will take longer, so be mindful of this. If the top looks like it's browning too quickly, you can cover the surface of the cheesecake with a piece of aluminum foil to prevent it from browning further. The cheesecake layer should be set (if you shake the pan, it won't jiggle). Cool the cheesecake completely, then place in the fridge for several hours or overnight so that it's nice and cold: they are best served chilled.

Storing: The brownies last for just about a week if stored in the fridge.

Roasted Rhubarb

Prep time: 5 min
Cook time: 25 min
Serves: 6–8

Ingredients

500 g / 17.6 oz rhubarb (around 5 medium-sized stalks)

2 teaspoons orange zest (optional)

100 g / 3.5 oz granulated sugar (plus more if needed)

1 tablespoon cornstarch

Juice of one orange (approximately 3 tablespoons)

I wanted to include a recipe for rhubarb in the book—something that was easy to put together, allowing you to quickly use up any stalks that you might have purchased during a trip to the market or store. This one works well as a topping for ice cream (pictured), whipped cream, pancakes, vanilla cake, or scones and is also lovely in a trifle (see below). It takes minutes to prepare, is pretty much foolproof, and is a wonderful way to use rhubarb!

Start by preheating the oven to 200°C or 390°F. Rinse the rhubarb stalks, trim off the tops and bottoms, then cut them into pieces around 1.5 to 2 cm (½ to ¾ inch) long. Lightly grease a baking dish with butter or oil, then throw in the rhubarb. Sprinkle on top of it the orange zest, sugar, and cornstarch, and give the ingredients a quick stir. Next, pour in the orange juice. Spread the rhubarb into an even layer and bake for 20 to 25 minutes or until the rhubarb has softened.

The rhubarb should be very tender and break apart easily.

Taste the mixture and add more sugar if it is still too sour. Serve this syrupy goodness warm, with some vanilla ice cream (my favorite), or perhaps with the orange olive oil cake (p. 83).

Storing: It will also last for several days in the fridge if stored properly, but make sure to heat it up before serving.

> *Note:*
> The Regal Mango Trifle (p. 93) is my go-to trifle recipe. For a rhubarb variation, replace the mango mixture with the roasted rhubarb (and make sure to keep all those beautiful juices!).

August

August is a bittersweet month for many. It is the last month of summer, and each day spent with family and friends is one to be cherished. Although the weather remains pleasant, hints of fall slowly begin to appear amid the vibrant summer produce. To me this is the best of both: each season is at its peak, yet figs, apples, and plums are also coming into their own.

The recipes I chose for the month of August pay tribute to all of the wonderful produce available this time of year. Baked Yogurt, a luscious, creamy pudding, is a perfect companion to virtually all fruit. It is delightful whether you serve it with figs or with peaches. The Apple and Cardamom Cake makes good use of apples, now in season, but this delicious, versatile cake can be made with other available fruit you love—apricots, perhaps strawberries if they are available, and cherries too. The same goes for the Ricotta and Plum Cake. And of course, you can never go wrong with a good Pear Crumble. I chose to use one of my favorites, pears, in the recipe, but any fruit will work: mixed berries, apples, rhubarb, peaches, and plums, all are delectable.

Baked Yogurt

Prep time: 5 min

Cooking time: 30 min

Makes: 6 servings

Ingredients

1 can (roughly 397 g / 14 oz / 1⅓ cups) sweetened condensed milk

330 mL / 11.2 fl oz (1⅓ cups) Greek-style yogurt

330 mL / 11.2 fl oz (1⅓ cups) heavy whipping cream

To serve:

A drizzle of honey

Figs or fresh fruit to garnish

A sister to cheesecake, these dainty little puddings are delicate, decadent, tangy, and sweet. Because the recipe is a 1:1:1 ingredient ratio, you can easily adjust it for how many portions you want to make. Its simple ingredients are a combination of thick, Greek-style yogurt (the star of the show), cream, and sweetened condensed milk—no eggs or gelatin are required, but it will cook and set beautifully, trust me. Out of all the recipes in this book, this is one I laud for its simplicity and taste. You'll be in awe.

Preheat the oven to 180°C or 350°F. Arrange 6 small ramekins or baking pots (8 to 10 cm, or 3 to 4 inches, in diameter) in a large roasting dish.

In a large bowl, mix together all the ingredients—the condensed milk, yogurt, and cream—until smooth. The mixture will be fairly thin, but it will thicken while baking. Using a ladle, divide the mixture between the ramekins, filling them around three-quarters full (this will be roughly 125 mL / 4.2 fl oz / ½ cup of the mixture). Place the roasting dish in the middle rack of your oven and fill it with boiling hot water from a kettle. The water should be enough to submerge the ramekins about halfway, but make sure that the water does not enter the ramekin itself. This hot water bath ensures that the puddings will have a velvety smooth consistency.

Bake the pots for about 25 to 30 minutes or until the mixture is set. If you move one ramekin just slightly, the interior shouldn't wobble. At this point, carefully remove the roasting dish from the oven (making sure that no water spills) and, using an oven mitt, remove the ramekins from the water. Be careful, as they will be hot. Let the puddings cool to room temperature. Next, cover the desserts with plastic wrap and place in the fridge for at least two hours or until they are cold to the touch.

Serve with honey and figs, or fruit of your choice.

Storing: Store these covered in the fridge for several days at most, without any garnish

Apple and Cardamom Cake

Prep time: 30 min

Cooking time: 30 min

Makes: around 8 slices

For the cake:

225 g / 7.9 oz (1½ cups) all-purpose flour

175 g / 6.2 oz (¾ cup) granulated sugar

½ teaspoon salt

2 teaspoons baking powder

1 teaspoon ground cardamom

75 mL / 2.5 fl oz (⅓ cup) vegetable oil

1 large egg

75 mL / 2.5 fl oz (⅓ cup) buttermilk (or alternatively ⅓ cup milk mixed with 1 tablespoon white or apple cider vinegar)

1 teaspoon vanilla extract

3 large apples (450 g / 15.9 oz whole), peeled, cored, and chopped into 1-cm or half-inch cubes

For the streusel topping:

50 g / 1.8 oz (¼ cup) unsalted butter, softened

70 g / 2.5 oz (⅓ cup) granulated sugar

1½ teaspoons ground cinnamon

1 teaspoon ground cardamom

¼ teaspoon salt

70 g / 2.5 oz (½ cup) all-purpose flour

During my "gap" semester between high school and university, I gave catering a try. One of the most popular cakes I made was this one, a tender, spiced cake speckled with bits of fresh apple. The hint of cardamom adds a unique but welcome flavor, leaving you with a craving for more. Cardamom is warm and can go alongside cinnamon and nutmeg in the spice aisle. The streusel topping is my favorite thing about this cake; a cinnamon-cardamom finish that gives the cake a nice crunch. You could also throw in some nuts, play a little more with the spices, or replace the apples with other fruit, such as pears or strawberries, for something a little different.

To begin, preheat the oven to 180°C or 350°F. Next, butter a 20-to-24-cm (8-to -9-inch) springform tin, then line the bottom with a circle of parchment paper and dust the sides of the tin with some extra flour to prevent sticking.

For the cake, mix the flour, sugar, salt, baking powder, and cardamom in a large bowl. Make a well in the center and add in the oil, egg, buttermilk, and vanilla. The batter will be quite thick. Fold in the chopped apples until just until incorporated (don't overwork the cake batter, as it will result in a denser cake), then pour the mixture into the prepared cake tin.

For the streusel topping, mix the butter with the sugar, cinnamon, cardamom, and salt. The mixture should be light, creamy, and fragrant. Next, toss in the flour. You should end up with a crumbly mixture that is the consistency of cookie dough but won't stick to your hands.

Distribute the mixture over the top of the cake as evenly as possible, then bake the cake for 45 to 60 minutes (depending on how big your cake tin is), checking every now and then after the 45-minute mark until a toothpick inserted comes out mostly clean with a few damp crumbs. If you notice the top browning too quickly in the oven, slide in a piece of aluminum foil over the cake pan. This will prevent it from burning.

Let the cake cool, then run a knife around the edges to loosen it and unmold it from the springform tin. This cake tastes delicious warm, but unmolding it while still hot may prove a challenge. Your call.

Right before serving, you can peel off the parchment paper from the bottom. I like to serve the cake warm or at room temperature with a dusting of confectioners' sugar. It's lovely plain, or with a little whipped cream or ice cream.

Storing: The cake lasts for several days if stored in the fridge, but because it has fruit, it's best eaten fresh.

Ricotta and Plum Cake

Prep time: 25 min

Cook time: 35–40 min

Makes: 8 slices

For the cake:

425 g / 15 oz fresh plums (around 10–12), thickly sliced

175 g / 6.2 oz (¾ cup) granulated sugar

1 tablespoon lemon zest (zest from around one and a half lemons)

80 mL / 2.7 fl oz (⅓ cup) olive oil

250 g / 8.8 oz (1 cup) ricotta cheese

2 large eggs

225 g / 7.9 oz (1½ cup) all-purpose flour

2 teaspoons baking powder

1 teaspoon salt

Topping:

25 g / 0.9 oz (2 tablespoons) unsalted butter, softened at room temperature

2 tablespoons brown sugar

50 g / 1.8 oz (⅔ cup) flaked almonds

Confectioners' sugar for dusting

When I had just started university, my friend Maya had a surplus of fruit in her possession, courtesy of her father. I and several other of her friends were the fortunate recipients of succulent French plums. I decided to combine the fruit in a cake, along with ricotta cheese, olive oil, and lemon zest (things I already had in the fridge). The end result was an incredibly tender cake, with subtle lemon and olive oil undertones. The juicy plums provide a nice burst of freshness, a tribute to the end of summer. The cake itself will work with a variety of other fruit as well, but the combination of ricotta, lemon, and plum is unbeatable.

To make the cake, first preheat the oven to 180°C or 350°F and generously butter a 22-cm (9-inch) circular springform cake tin. Then line the bottom with a circle of parchment paper and dust the sides of the tin with some extra flour to prevent sticking. Next, prepare the plums. Run your knife around the center of the plum, then twist to release the halves from the core. If the core is tough, you will just need to cut around it until you can remove it from the center. Slice each half, creating slices around ½-¾ cm or ¼ to ⅓ inch in thickness. Once you've sliced all the plums, set aside.

In a large bowl, combine the sugar and lemon zest: the zest should be well-dispersed throughout the mixture. Next, pour in the olive oil, followed by the ricotta cheese and the eggs, mixing till the batter is nice and smooth. In a medium-sized bowl, stir together the flour, baking powder, and salt. Gently mix the dry ingredients with the wet, just until combined.

Pour the batter into the prepared pan, and arrange the plums on top of the cake. I like to do this neatly in a circular motion and cover the entirety of the surface.

For the topping and baking:

To make the topping, mix together the butter and brown sugar in a small bowl, using the back of a spoon. Gently stir in the almonds, but be careful not to break them. Dollop the mixture in ½-teaspoon-sized mounds over the top of the cake, as evenly as possible.

Bake the cake for 35 to 40 minutes or until a toothpick inserted into the cake portion (not the plum) comes out clean. Let the cake cool for 10 to 15 minutes, then run a knife around the edges. Loosen the cake from the springform tin. I also release the bottom using a spatula. Then place the cake on a cake plate or board. Dust with a little confectioners' sugar before serving.

Storing: This cake will last up to a week if stored in the fridge and sealed properly. Bring to room temperature before serving.

Pear Crumble

Prep time: 30 min

Cook time: 40–45 min

Makes: 6–8 servings

For the pears:

6 ripe pears (600–700 g / 21.2–24.7 oz
/ 6 cups), cut, cored and cubed into
1-cm (½-inch) pieces*

1 tablespoon lemon juice

1 tablespoon cornstarch (optional)

For the crumble topping:

50 g / 1.8 oz (½ cup) walnuts (optional)

150 g / 5.3 oz (1 cup) all-purpose flour

50 g / 1.8 oz (½ cup) whole rolled oats

100 g / 3.5 oz (½ cup) brown sugar

½ teaspoon salt

125 g / 4.4 oz (½ cup) cold unsalted
butter, cut into small cubes

To serve:

Vanilla ice cream

If there's one recipe that should get you started with baking, it's a crumble. It is foolproof in preparation, beyond delicious in taste, and works well with virtually any kind of fruit. I've tried this recipe with apples and raspberries, plums, rhubarb, and peaches, and all work beautifully. Just be sure to note that each fruit has a different level of sweetness, so you may need to add several spoonfuls of sugar to amplify the taste. Pears require little to no added sugar as their natural sweet, syrupy flavor necessitates very few additions. You'll want to serve this pear crumble in generous portions, with a nice scoop of vanilla ice cream.

Preheat the oven to 180°C or 350°F and generously line a 24-to-26-cm (9-to-10-inch) baking dish with butter. I like to use a ceramic dish and serve the crumble from it, but don't be too worried about the precise size of the pan, as long as it fits all the pears with adequate room for the crumb topping.

If you haven't already, peel the pears, then cut them into quarters, making sure to remove the core. The pears should be ripe, so that they soften while baking. Additionally, the sweeter the pears, the better the crumble, since no sugar goes into the fruit portion. Roughly chop the pears into pieces around 1.5 cm (⅔ inch) big. Next, tip the pears into a medium-sized bowl, and sprinkle the lemon juice and cornstarch on top. The cornstarch helps thicken the pear juices, but I've also made this recipe without it and it works fine. Mix the ingredients together until well-combined. Spoon the pear mixture into your prepared baking dish and set aside.

To make the crumble, begin by chopping the nuts into small pieces (the size of mini chocolate chips). Tip the nuts into a medium-sized bowl, along with the flour, oats, brown sugar, and salt. Add the butter to the mixture and work it in, using a fork or a pastry cutter, until thoroughly combined. The mixture should resemble a coarse dough but should still clump together slightly. Using your fingers, spread the crumble mixture evenly on top of the fruit, breaking up the larger clumps. Put into the oven and bake till the edges are bubbly and the top is a beautiful golden brown, around 40 to 45 min. Let the crumble cool for several minutes before serving.

Enjoy this warm, with some ice cream.

Storing: Although this stores well for a few days if refrigerated, it does get a bit soggy. So the crumble is best straight from the oven, when the crumble topping is nice and crisp.

Note: If the pears are not ripe or sweet enough, add 1 to 2 tablespoons of sugar or even maple syrup to sweeten the crumble.

September

When the weather grows colder, the leaves turn shades of gold, brown, and red. Jackets, sweaters, hats, gloves, and boots begin to appear, and the aisles of the grocery store are stocked with an abundance of squash and pumpkins, along with apples, pears, and other seasonal produce. I have been extremely privileged to enjoy fall in two countries that experience it beautifully, Poland and the Netherlands.

It is my favorite time of year and always has been. For one, I have a particular affinity for boots and sweaters over other items of clothing, and I love having an excuse to go for a hot chocolate or a cappuccino at the café around the corner with friends. And of course, there's the baking. Fall provides a welcome excuse to turn on the oven: baking brings warmth and comfort, characteristics that are needed as the days grow shorter and colder.

But fall is also associated with a certain freshness, since it brings the beginning of the school year and people are rejuvenated after the long summer days. Caffeine Infusion Mocha Muffins are the perfect way to jump-start those mornings if you need some extra energy. My Peanut Butter and Jelly Crumb Bars join the classic flavors of peanut butter and jelly for a fantastic dessert bar that even works for a breakfast treat.

In addition, I am particularly enticed by the seasonal produce this time of year—apples, pears, pumpkins, and courgette, which go so well with spices like cinnamon, nutmeg, cloves, and cardamom. These are the flavors that make up this chapter, as well as my Classic Apple Pie, something I can't seem to get enough of. The Courgette Cake is fluffy and soft, like a carrot cake. It might seem a bit outlandish, but give it a try.

Caffeine Infusion Muffins

Prep time: 20 min

Cook time: 20–25 min

Makes: 10–11 muffins

For the muffins:

120 mL / 4.1 fl oz (½ cup) whole milk

2 tablespoons instant espresso powder

1 large egg

6 tablespoons (90 mL / 3 fl oz) vegetable oil

1 teaspoon vanilla extract

225 g / 7.9 oz (1½ cups) all-purpose flour

150 g / 5.3 oz (¾ cup) granulated sugar

1 teaspoon baking powder

1 teaspoon ground cinnamon

½ teaspoon salt

100 g / 3.5 oz (⅔ cup) dark chocolate, chopped

For the glaze:

150 g / 5.3 oz (1 cup) confectioners' sugar

½ teaspoon instant espresso powder (optional)

1½–2 tablespoons water or milk

½ teaspoon vanilla extract

It isn't easy to return to a proper routine after months of lazing about during the summer. These muffins might help ease the transition from vacation mode to work mode: you can get your caffeine fix and begin your day on a slightly sweeter note. These muffins are ridiculously easy to throw together and make for a much-appreciated lunchbox treat. If you prefer a caffeine-free version, you can substitute decaf alternatives.

Preheat the oven to 180°C or 350°F and line a muffin tray with paper liners, enough for 14 muffins. You can also just grease the wells with butter and dust with flour if you do not have paper liners. In a small saucepan or in the microwave, whisk together the milk and the instant espresso powder, until the espresso powder is completely dissolved in the milk.

Pour the milk-coffee mixture into a medium bowl or jug and let it cool completely. At this point, whisk in the egg, oil, and vanilla.

Next, in a large bowl, stir together the flour, sugar, baking powder, cinnamon, and salt until smooth. Make a well in the center of the dry ingredients and then pour in the milk-espresso mixture. Gently stir the batter until well-combined, but don't overmix, as that will result in a tougher muffin. Finally, fold in the dark chocolate.

Using an ice cream scoop or a spoon, fill the muffin tins about ⅔ of the way with the batter. Bake for around 22 to 27 minutes or until a toothpick inserted comes out relatively clean, but be careful not to pierce a piece of the chocolate. Cool slightly before serving. In the meantime, prepare the glaze.

To make the glaze, stir together the sugar and espresso powder, then trickle in the water or milk until the mixture is smooth. The more milk you add, the runnier the glaze will be. Once you're satisfied with the consistency, add in the vanilla extract.

Dip the top of muffins in the glaze, allowing it to drip down the sides slightly.

Storing: These are best enjoyed warm of course, but you can keep them for a week if sealed properly, preferably in the fridge, or longer if stored without the glaze.

Peanut Butter and Jelly Bars

Prep time: 10-15 min

Cook time: 25-30 min

Makes: 8

Ingredients

½ teaspoon salt

½ teaspoon baking soda

225 g / 7.9 oz (1½ cups) all-
purpose flour

100 g / 3.5 oz (1 cup) whole rolled oats

125 g / 4.4 oz (½ cup) unsalted butter,
soft at room temperature

150 g / 5.3 oz (¾ cup) peanut butter*

100 g / 3.5 oz (½ cup) brown sugar

50 g / 1.8 oz (¼ cup) granulated sugar

1 large egg

1 teaspoon vanilla extract

Handful of peanuts, roughly chopped
(optional)

100 g / 3.5 oz (⅔ cup) dark chocolate
(50 percent cacao solids), roughly
chopped (optional)*

230 g / 8.1 oz (⅔ cup) strawberry jam
(or jam of your preference)

This recipe is reminiscent of the classic peanut butter and jelly sandwich I used to enjoy at school. If I were still in grade school, this is a recipe I would make for one of the bake sales that often took place, or to share with my friends. It makes for a delicious lunchbox treat and is a favorite of peanut butter lovers. The peanut butter dough recipe is perfection in itself, so if you prefer to make it in cookie form instead, roll the dough into 1½ inch balls and bake them for 11 to 13 minutes.

Preheat the oven to 180°C or 350°F and line a 22x22-cm (9x9-inch) square tin, or something of a similar size, with parchment paper, and set aside. In a bowl, whisk together the salt, baking soda, flour, and oats and set aside.

In a large bowl, cream together the butter and peanut butter with the sugars until smooth and well-combined. Add in the egg and vanilla extract, continuing to whisk. Next, stir in the dry ingredients, using a wooden spoon or spatula, until the mixture comes together into a thick dough. Finally, add in the chopped peanuts and chocolate, if using.

Press around ⅔ of the mixture onto the bottom of the prepared cake tin. Next, spread the jam on top, reaching all the corners. Crumble the remaining dough with your fingertips, and scatter it atop the jam layer, covering as much surface area as possible. Bake for 25 to 30 minutes, or until the top is golden.

Remove the tray from the oven. Although these bars taste heavenly while still warm, they are easier to cut when completely cooled. If you would like to use these for a bake sale or something similar, I would recommend making them a day in advance and chilling them in the fridge. This ensures a firmer, sturdier consistency.

Storing: These store for about a week if sealed properly and refrigerated.

Notes:

♦ I made this recipe using smooth and/or chunky peanut butter, which is thicker and creamier in consistency than the all-natural kind. Feel free to use the latter, but it might result in a slightly different flavor and texture.

♦ I like chocolate in this recipe and feel it balances the sweetness of the jam well, but some of my taste testers prefer these bars without it.

Classic Apple Pie

Prep time: 1 hour (including making the crust)

Cook time: 45 min–1 hour

Makes: 1 large pie, about 8 slices

For the crust:

makes enough for one pie

350 g / 12.3 oz (2 ½ cups) cups all-purpose flour

1 tbsp granulated sugar

2 tsp salt

225 g / 7.9 oz / 1 cup butter

8–12 tbsp ice water*

For the filling:

5–6 apples, peeled, cored, and sliced (6 cups / 325 g / 11.5 oz)

1 lemon, juiced (3 tablespoons)

100 g / 3.5 oz (½ cup) sugar, either brown or granulated is fine

1 teaspoon ground cinnamon

½ teaspoon ground nutmeg

3 tablespoons all-purpose flour

½ teaspoon salt

1 tablespoon unsalted butter

1 large egg + 1 tablespoon water for the egg wash; alternatively, use heavy whipping cream

1–2 tablespoons granulated sugar for sprinkling

If I had to select one dessert as the symbol of fall, it would be this one. The scent of apples baking with cinnamon and nutmeg wafting through the kitchen is undeniably uplifting and comforting. When I was younger, I attended an apple pie-making workshop at school, led by one of the American teachers on UN Day, a multicultural event to celebrate the various countries that people were from. There is something very comforting about making a pie. It is time-consuming, but an incredibly therapeutic process. Apple pie is something I have chosen over cake on my birthday, a recipe that I return to over and over again.

For the filling:

To make the filling, toss the apple slices in lemon juice (to prevent them from browning) in a large bowl. In a smaller bowl, stir together the sugar, cinnamon, nutmeg, flour, and salt till well-combined. Toss the apples in the spice mixture, then set aside while you assemble the pie.

Next, preheat the oven to 200°C or 390°F and grease a 22-to-24-cm (9-to-10-inch) circular pie dish with butter. Divide the dough for the crust into two portions, one slightly bigger than the other. On a lightly floured work surface, roll the bigger portion into a circle about 30 cm (15 inches) in diameter. Gently lift the dough circle and place it into the pie dish, until it entirely coats the bottom and sides. It's okay if extra crust hangs over the edge—you can trim it later. Fill the prepared crust with the apples. Using your fingers, break the tablespoon of butter into bitesize pieces (the size of peas) and dot the top of the pie with the butter. This keeps the apples juicy.

Now, roll out the second disk. If you want to do a lattice top as depicted in the photos, use a pizza cutter or knife to cut across the crust to form strips, about 2 to 3 cm (1 inch) thick.

Lay the strips on top of the pie in a parallel arrangement, about 1 to 1½ inches apart. Then, fold back every other strip, about halfway. Place another strip perpendicular to the parallel strips, and fold over the strips that you had folded back. Fold back the other strips (the ones that haven't been folded yet), and lay another strip perpendicular to the folded strips, but parallel to the last perpendicular one. Continue to repeat this process until the pie has been latticed completely on one side, then repeat with the other side. It's difficult to explain the process in words, so make sure to look at the pictures!

Brush the top of the pie with the beaten egg/water mixture, and sprinkle the top evenly with the sugar. Bake the pie for 45 to 50 min or until the top is golden and the filling is bubbly, then cool for about 20 minutes before serving. Serve with some ice cream (or it's actually a known practice in the US to eat a piece of pie with a slice of cheddar cheese, if you're feeling a little adventurous).

Storing: This lasts up to a week stored in the fridge and tastes delicious warm or cold.

For the crust:

Prepare the crust, place the butter in the freezer around 30 min before using.

In the meantime, mix together the flour, sugar, and salt using a fork or pastry blender, and chill in the fridge if time allows (the colder your ingredients, the flakier the crust will be).

Using the larger portion of a box grater, roughly grate the butter. You can also chop it into small cubes.

Work the butter into the flour mixture, either with a fork or a pastry cutter, until you're left with small, pea-sized bits of butter dispersed within the flour. Grating the butter makes it easier to mix, so using cubes of butter may require a bit of elbow grease. The mixture should resemble the texture of uneven breadcrumbs. It doesn't need to be too fine.

Mix in the ice water using the fork/pastry cutter. Add 8 tbsp first, and then 1 tbsp at a time until the mixture comes together. You'll form the dough into a ball using your hands, but be careful not to overwork the mixture! You want to keep the overall temperature of the dough cool, so that the butter does not melt into it. This helps with the crust's flakiness.

Divide the dough into two portions and wrap each portion in plastic wrap. Place the dough in the refrigerator for at least 1 hour before using, or in the freezer for 30 min.

Storing: You can freeze the dough for several months if wrapped tightly, then thaw in the fridge before using.

Courgette Cake with Chocolate Ganache

Prep time: 20 min

Cook time: 1 hour

Makes: 8–10 servings

For the cake:

225 g / 7.9 oz (1½ cups) all-purpose flour

175 g / 6.2 oz (¾ cup) granulated sugar

1 teaspoon baking powder

½ teaspoon baking soda

1 teaspoon salt

1 teaspoon ground cinnamon

½ teaspoon ground nutmeg

6 tablespoons vegetable oil

225 g / 7.9 oz (1 cup, packed) courgette (zucchini), about half a large one, finely shredded

1 teaspoon vanilla extract

6 tablespoons plain yogurt

For the chocolate ganache:

100 g / 3.5 oz (⅔ cup) dark chocolate (62 percent cacao solids), roughly chopped

125 mL / 4.2 fl oz (½ cup) heavy whipping cream

½ teaspoon instant espresso powder

To finish:

Handful of shelled, finely chopped, unsalted pistachios

If you enjoy a carrot cake (see p. 85) or a pumpkin cake (see p. 155), you'll love this recipe. The courgette (zucchini) provides a soft, tender crumb to this cake, and no one will be able to decipher that mysterious ingredient. This cake is also egg-free, meaning that it can be made vegan if you use a non-dairy yogurt such as soy. This recipe also makes the fluffiest, softest muffins and makes for a nice lunchtime treat or end to a brunch. For a more decadent, stylish finish, coat the cake with chocolate ganache and decorate with chopped nuts.

To make the cake, preheat the oven to 180°C or 350°F and grease a 22-cm (9-inch) loaf tin with butter, then dust it with flour, or use a loaf liner. Set aside.

In a large bowl, mix together the flour, sugar, baking powder, baking soda, salt, cinnamon, and nutmeg using a whisk or spatula. Next, make a well in the center of the mixture and add the oil, shredded zucchini, vanilla extract, and yogurt, and mix till smooth. Do not overmix, as this will overwork the gluten in the cake and result in a tougher crumb.

Pour the mixture into your prepared cake tin and bake for around an hour (you might need 5 to 10 minutes more) or until a toothpick inserted comes out clean. Let the cake cool completely before glazing.

To make the ganache, place the chocolate into a medium-sized bowl and set aside. Bring the cream to a boil, either by heating it in a saucepan over medium heat along with the espresso powder, or by placing it in the microwave for about 1 to 2 minutes. Pour the cream over the chopped chocolate and let the mixture sit for about 30 seconds. Using a whisk, mix everything together until it is smooth and let it cool slightly.

To assemble the cake, pour the ganache over the top of the cake, using a spoon to help it drip down the sides. Sprinkle some of the chopped pistachios on top and serve warm or at room temperature.

Storing: This cake keeps well for about a week at room temperature if sealed properly, and up to two weeks in the fridge, but like most cakes, is best served fresh.

October

With winter's festivities just around the corner, spirits in October are high, a month of fun and anticipation. Special occasions mark the calendar, such as Halloween, Thanksgiving, and Diwali, that give you a reason to stock up on baking essentials such as flour and sugar and create something festive.

In this section, the fusion of seasonal pumpkin and chai flavors in my Pumpkin Chai Cupcakes brings together India and the Western world. Next, *Gajar ka Halwa,* a comforting carrot pudding, is a traditional Indian dessert, something to serve up during Diwali, but can also be enjoyed any time of year. Its vibrant orange color also makes it a unique and delicious Halloween treat or festive ending to any fall meal.

Also included in this section is a recipe for *Kalakand,* Indian milk fudge, a traditional Indian *mithai* or sweet that is sure to please. Last is the Cinnamon Roll Cake, a warm fall dessert perfect for the season. All of these recipes are delightfully easy to make, insanely good, and sure to be new favorites.

Pumpkin Chai Spice Cupcakes with Dark Chocolate Ganache

Prep time: 30 min

Cook time: 20 min

Makes: 12 cupcakes

For the cupcakes:

250 g / 8.8 oz (1 cup) pumpkin puree*

200 g / 7.1 oz (1 cup) sugar (brown, raw, or granulated sugar all work fine)

125 mL / 4.2 fl oz (½ cup) flavorless oil such as canola or vegetable

1 large egg

150 g / 5.3 oz (1 cup) all-purpose flour

1½ teaspoons baking powder

1 teaspoon baking soda

1 teaspoon cinnamon*

½ teaspoon ground cardamom

½ teaspoon ground ginger

¼ teaspoon nutmeg

¼ teaspoon ground cloves or allspice

A pinch of black pepper

A pinch of salt

50 g / 1.8 oz (½ cup) unsalted walnuts

For the frosting:

200 g / 7.1 oz (1¼ cups) dark chocolate (at least 50 percent cacao solids), roughly chopped

1 tablespoon unsalted butter

1 teaspoon instant espresso powder

A pinch of salt

200 mL / 6.8 fl oz (¾ cup + 2 tablespoons) heavy whipping cream (around 36 percent fat solids)

Cranberries, pumpkin seeds, or sprinkles for topping

When I was six, I could recite the entire Cinderella story by heart. I loved it so much. I guess a part of it has stuck with me all these years, because my favorite fall vegetable is pumpkin. Around October, pumpkin maneuvers its way into nearly all my meals. My friends tease me, and eye me hesitantly when I blend pumpkin into everything from pasta, curry, and risotto to cookies and cupcakes. In the end, though, they always approve. Pumpkin is a treasure, and works like magic in so many different recipes, every single time. This pumpkin cupcake recipe yields an incredibly flavorful cupcake, with a soft, tender crumb. The nuts add a nice crunch but can be omitted. Give this recipe a try, and I promise you'll be amazed. And, in case you too decide to make pumpkin your go-to fall vegetable, I've listed my favorite way to make fresh pumpkin puree below. Keep it in the fridge or freeze it, and add it to your meals, whenever you have an urge to do so.

To make the cupcakes, preheat the oven to 180°C or 350°F and line a cupcake tray with paper liners. In a medium-sized bowl, combine the pumpkin puree, sugar, oil, and egg, beating until smooth.

In a separate bowl, combine the flour, baking powder, baking soda, cinnamon, cardamom, ginger, nutmeg, cloves or allspice, black pepper, salt, and walnuts. Stir the dry ingredients into the wet ones until your batter is smooth. Don't overmix, as that will yield a tougher cupcake by overworking the gluten in the flour. Fill the paper liners ¾ of the way full: these make exactly 12. Bake the cupcakes for 20 to 22 minutes, or until a toothpick inserted comes out clean, then let them cool for five minutes and remove them from the tin. Let the cupcakes cool completely before frosting, for around 30 minutes.

For the frosting, place the chocolate into a heatproof bowl, along with the butter, instant espresso powder, and salt. Heat the heavy whipping cream until it is almost at a boil, either in the microwave or over the stovetop. Pour the heavy whipping cream over the chocolate mixture and let it sit for around 30 seconds. Next, whisk the ingredients together until smooth. Chill the ganache until it is firm enough to pipe, for around an hour. The darker the chocolate, the quicker the ganache will solidify. Spread or pipe the ganache onto the cupcakes, and top with sprinkles, pumpkin seeds, or dried cranberries for a bit of color.

Storing: You can store the cupcakes, sealed, for up to a week in the fridge or at room temperature unfrosted, and for several days in the refrigerator after frosting. These are best enjoyed at room temperature.

Tip: To make your own pumpkin puree, you'll need a sweet, flavorful pumpkin to make your own puree. I like to use a sugar pumpkin or a Hokkaido pumpkin, a small, bright orange squash that is to die for. Cut the pumpkin in half and scrape out all the seeds. Place each half cut-side down onto a parchment-lined baking tray, and into a 200°C (390°F) oven for about 40 to 50 minutes or until you can pierce a fork through one of the halves easily. The longer you bake the pumpkin, the softer they will be for the puree. Once the pumpkin is cooked, let it cool, then scrape out the flesh and mash (if it's soft enough and not stringy), or puree in a blender or food processor.

Note: Any of the nuts or spices can be left out.

Gajar Halwa (Indian Carrot Pudding)

Prep time: 20 min

Cook time: 3–3½ hours

Makes: 4–5 servings

Ingredients

500 g / 17.6 oz (4 cups) carrots, peeled and grated*

1 L (around 4½ cups) whole milk (4 percent fat)*

1 tablespoon ghee (clarified butter), or alternatively use regular butter*

A handful of cashews (optional, can also replace with almonds or pistachios)

A handful of raisins (optional)

100 g / 3.5 oz (½ cup) granulated sugar

½ teaspoon ground cardamom*

A pinch of salt

Additional chopped nuts to garnish

Gajar Halwa is one of the most popular desserts in India, a delicious way to use vibrant red carrots (a color I haven't seen anywhere else in Europe). I wanted to include *gajar halwa* in the October section of this book because the color of the pudding seems fitting not only for Diwali, the Indian festival of lights, but also for Halloween. Each Indian household has its own version, some with more *ghee* (clarified butter) or nuts, or different sugar ratios, but this recipe is my family's favorite.

In a large heavy-duty pot, add the carrots followed by the milk, and place over medium heat. Bring the mixture to a boil, stirring gently—it will take around 5 min. Reduce the flame to low, and let the carrots and milk cook, stirring every 10 minutes or so. What you want is for *all* the milk to evaporate. This takes me 3 hours and 15 minutes in total, but it depends on the heat: a higher heat will take less time (and more frequent stirring), a lower heat may take even more time. However, the longer the cooking time, the more delicate and delicious the *halwa* will be.

When the *halwa* seems close to being done (after around 2 hours and 45 minutes), prepare the nuts and raisins. Warm the ghee in a small frying pan, and add in the cashews and raisins. Shake the frying pan to cook evenly, till the cashews begin to turn a light brown, then turn off the heat. Add the sugar, cardamom, and salt to the carrot mixture, stirring slowly for a minute or so or until the sugar has dissolved, followed by the nuts and the ghee (don't discard any of it!). Let the *halwa* cook with all the ingredients until all the milk has completely evaporated. It should be very thick, as no liquid should be left, and slightly glossy.

Let the *halwa* cool for around 10 minutes before serving, and garnish with additional chopped nuts. We like to enjoy this delicacy hot, in rather small quantities. You can serve it with a bit of vanilla ice cream too, if you like.

Storing: This keeps for a week or so in the fridge, stored in an airtight container. Make sure to warm it up before eating.

Notes:

♦ Feel free to add more milk or *ghee* for a creamier, richer pudding, more sugar for a sweeter version, or more cardamom or nuts, as you see fit.

♦ Grate the carrots using the smaller part of your box grater (as you would grate parmesan cheese, resembling vermicelli).

♦ Using full-fat milk makes it richer and tastier. You can try substituting dairy-free alternatives to make this recipe vegan, such as cashew milk or almond milk. You can also try this recipe with vegan butter or coconut oil.

Kalakand (Indian Milk and Cardamom Fudge)

Prep time: 15 min

Cook time: 1 hour

Makes: 35–48 pieces

Ingredients

2 tablespoons unsalted butter

1 can (roughly 397 g / 14 oz) sweetened condensed milk

500 g / 17.6 oz (2 cups) ricotta cheese

¼ teaspoon ground cardamom*

A pinch of salt

200 g / 7.1 oz unsalted, shelled pistachios, almonds, or a mix, finely crushed

One of my most cherished memories of living in India was celebrating Diwali, the Hindu festival of lights, which takes place in October. On Diwali, everyone would come together to light firecrackers and share Indian confections, such as *kalakand*, milk fudge. Traditional *kalakand* requires the separation of milk, and then cooking the curds slowly with more milk and sugar. My recipe is a cheat version—it cuts the recipe time in half and calls for fewer ingredients but is just as good. The cooking process still takes around an hour, but you can tinker around with other kitchen-related business in the meantime. *Kalakand* is made with a touch of cardamom, which is optional, but highly recommended. This recipe simply takes me home.

Line a 22-cm (9-inch) square dish with aluminum foil, and grease the foil with melted butter. You can also use parchment paper. Add the butter to a medium-sized pot over medium heat. Next, pour in the condensed milk and ricotta cheese, and combine them with a wooden spoon or rubber spatula. Stir every now and then until the mixture comes to a boil.

At this stage, reduce the heat to a low flame and let the mixture cook, stirring occasionally, until it has reduced in volume and has thickened significantly. The texture should resemble that of ricotta cheese (before using it in this recipe, of course), and the mixture should start to leave the sides of the pan. This should take around an hour. Next, stir in the cardamom and the salt.

Pour the mixture into the prepared dish, and sprinkle the nuts on top, pressing them into the mixture gently. Refrigerate the *kalakand* until it has solidified, for around 1 hour.

Cut into small squares and serve.

Storing: This keeps well for a week if stored properly in the fridge.

Note: For a more prominent cardamom flavor, use cardamom pods and grind using a mortar and pestle until they form a powder. Discard the skins and use the powder.

Cinnamon Roll Cake

Prep time: 25 min
Cook time: 20–25 min
Makes: 8–10 servings

For the cake:
225 g / 7.9 oz (1½ cups) all-purpose flour
2 teaspoons baking powder
½ teaspoon salt
110 g / 3.9 oz (½ cup) granulated sugar or brown sugar
175 mL / 5.9 fl oz (¾ cup) milk*
50 g / 1.8 oz (¼ cup) unsalted butter, melted
1 teaspoon vanilla extract
1 large egg

For the cinnamon-swirl mixture:
100 g / 3.5 oz (½ cup) unsalted butter, soft at room temperature
90 g / 3.2 oz (½ cup) brown sugar
75 g / 2.6 oz (⅔ cup) walnuts, finely chopped (optional)
1 tablespoon all-purpose flour
2 teaspoons ground cinnamon

For the glaze:
150 g / 5.3 oz (1 cup) confectioners' sugar
1 teaspoon vanilla extract
2 tablespoons milk*
Pinch of salt

When I was in high school, I used to be part of the running team which trained during the fall. Occasionally on Saturdays or Sundays, we'd go for long runs and then enjoy homemade cinnamon rolls that our coach would prepare. One Saturday, I decided to make this cinnamon roll cake to share with the team. It is a buttery vanilla cake swirled with cinnamon sugar and drizzled with a vanilla glaze that is lovely when eaten warm from the oven. This recipe has been tweaked and modified over the years and is now perfection itself. It is the embodiment of comfort food and is sure to be a crowd-pleaser.

To make the cake, preheat the oven to 180°C or 350°F, then butter and flour a 20x20-cm cake tin (8x8-inch), or something approximately that size (slightly bigger is fine too). I like to use a square or rectangular tin, but circular is just fine as well! Whisk together the flour, baking powder, salt, and sugar. Make a well in the center of the mixture and pour in the milk, melted butter, vanilla, and egg. Stir the mixture together until it is well-incorporated, then pour into your prepared pan. The batter may seem like not enough, but the cake rises quite a bit during baking.

For the cinnamon-swirl mixture, stir together the butter and brown sugar until smooth. Add in the chopped nuts, flour, and cinnamon, and continue to stir till smooth. Scoop 1-tablespoon-sized mounds of the mixture and scatter them across the cake. Then, run a butter knife across the cake several times to swirl the mixture.

Bake the cake for 25 to 30 minutes or until the center is set and a toothpick pierced into the cake part (not the cinnamon) comes out nearly clean, with a few moist crumbs. Let the cake cool slightly. In the meantime, prepare the glaze.

To make the glaze, stir together the sugar, vanilla, and milk until smooth.

Drizzle the glaze over the cake and serve it warm, while it is still gooey.

Storing: The cake also stores well if kept chilled in the fridge for up to a week.

Note: I use whole milk, but you can use 2 percent milk or a non-dairy alternative such as soy milk or almond milk.

November

By November, the days are growing shorter and colder and winter holidays are in the air. The occasional snowfall might be a welcome surprise. I love November firstly because it happens to be my birthday month, and it also means that December and the festivities the end of the year brings are just around the corner.

The range of recipes I have selected for November pay tribute to celebratory comfort food. Each dessert is bold, brilliant, and carries a certain warmth fitting for the season.

Mini Banana Cakes with Salted Caramel and Pecans provide a beautiful blend of sweet, salty, crunchy, and gooey. I can only describe it as seductive and warn you that anyone who tries it will be enchanted. If you celebrate Thanksgiving or just love pumpkin, give the Pumpkin Cheesecake a try—it is a brilliant combination of warm spices and a lush, creamy cheesecake, fit for festive gatherings. If you're in the mood for a dark, sumptuous chocolate dessert, the Silky Chocolate Pie recipe is the perfect choice: a velvety chocolate pudding encased in a dark chocolate cookie crust. Finally, the Pear *Tarte Tatin*, a French wonder, brings a medley of flavors using very few ingredients. It is pure gold, literally and figuratively.

Mini Banana Cakes with Salted Caramel and Pecans

Prep time: 30 min

Cook time: 30 min

Makes: 10–12 cakes

For the muffins:

3 very ripe bananas (roughly 325 g / 11.5 oz / 1½ cups, mashed)—the riper, the sweeter, the better!

75 g / 2.6 oz (⅓ cup) butter, melted (alternatively use oil)

100 g / 3.5 oz (½ cup) sugar (brown or granulated, both work fine)

1 large egg

1 teaspoon baking soda

½ teaspoon salt

1 teaspoon vanilla extract

225 g / 7.9 oz (1½ cups) all-purpose flour

100 g / 3.5 oz (¾ cup) dark chocolate, chopped (optional)

For the topping:

150 g / 5.3 oz (1 cup) unsalted pecans (alternatively, walnuts or hazelnuts work well too!)

3 tablespoons water

225 g / 7.9 oz (1 cup) granulated sugar

1 tablespoon butter (salted or unsalted, both work fine)

125 mL / 4.2 fl oz (½ cup) heavy whipping cream

1 teaspoon salt (plus extra if you want a saltier caramel)

1 teaspoon vanilla extract (optional)

Inspired by the English sticky toffee pudding, this is a simple banana bread recipe, drenched in the best salted caramel sauce and served with lightly toasted pecans for a nice crunch. Not only is this a personal favorite, it also does ridiculously well with my friends.

To make the muffins, preheat the oven to 180°C or 350°F and generously grease a 12-cup muffin tray with butter (you can also use paper liners to make clean-up a bit easier). To make this recipe in a 22-cm cake pan just adjust the baking time.

In a medium-sized bowl, mash the bananas with a fork. Stir in the melted butter, followed by the sugar, egg, baking soda, salt, vanilla, and flour, until the mixture is thick and smooth. Finally, stir in the chocolate, if using it. Divide the batter between the muffin cups, spooning them about ¾ of the way full.

Bake the muffins for about 20 to 25 minutes, or until a toothpick inserted comes out clean (if you're baking this as a single cake, it will take longer). Let the muffins cool for around 10 minutes, then run a knife around the edges to loosen them from the muffin tins. When cooled, twist them gently to release them from the cake pans.

To make the topping, toast the pecans by placing them on a parchment-lined baking sheet in an even layer and baking in a preheated 180°C (350°F) oven for 10 minutes or until lightly browned. To make the caramel, add the water and sugar to a small pan, then stir just to combine. Heat the pan over medium heat without stirring. You can swirl the pan. To prevent sugar crystals from forming on the sides, dip a pastry brush in some water and gently brush off the sides until the crystals are gone.

Just when the caramel becomes a bubbly amber color, turn off the heat. This should take 5 to 7 minutes. Be careful not to overcook, as burnt caramel is not tasty. Stand back (the mixture might splatter) and add the butter and heavy whipping cream. When the mixture calms down slightly, stir the ingredients until the sauce is silky smooth. If it separates, place the saucepan on low heat and stir the ingredients until they are combined.

Add the salt and vanilla and stir to taste. Stir the toasted pecans into the caramel sauce. Finally, spoon the mixture over the cooled muffins.

Storing: The cupcakes keep for around a week if stored and sealed properly in the fridge. The salted caramel keeps for several weeks if sealed and stored properly in the fridge. It can also be frozen for a longer duration. Once you top the cupcakes with salted caramel, try to eat them within a few days.

Pumpkin Cheesecake

Prep time: 30 min
Cook time: 1 hour
Makes: 6–8 slices

For the base:
250 g / 8.8 oz *Speculoos* (or alternatively gingersnap) cookies (2 cups of cookie crumbs, packed)
100 g / 3.5 oz (½ cup) unsalted butter, melted

For the filling:
450 g / 15.9 oz cream cheese, taken out of the fridge an hour or so before using
250 g / 8.8 oz (1 cup) pumpkin puree
3 large eggs
150 g / 5.3 oz (⅔ cup) granulated sugar
1 teaspoon vanilla extract
½ teaspoon ground cinnamon
¼ teaspoon ground nutmeg

For the topping:
250 mL / 8.5 fl oz (1 cup) heavy whipping cream
1 tablespoon granulated sugar
1 teaspoon vanilla extract
Salted caramel sauce (see p. 167 [where the banana muffins are]), optional, for topping
Handful of chopped walnuts and a touch of cinnamon, for garnish

If you're looking to stray away from a traditional pumpkin pie during pumpkin season, this majestic cheesecake is the way to go. It is tall, creamy, and encased in copious amounts of crust, courtesy of my sister, who thinks that the base makes or breaks the cheesecake. I honestly think that is fair enough. I use Dutch *Speculoos* cookies for this layer—they are ginger-cinnamon-infused cookies that mesh fabulously with the pumpkin, but chocolate cookies or simple digestives also pair well with the luscious pumpkin interior. This recipe is simple—no hot water bath or fancy techniques required. And if a much-dreaded crack appears on the surface, it is buried beneath a generous layer of whipped cream, so no one will know.

Preheat the oven to 180°C or 350°F and line the bottom of an 8-inch (20-cm springform pan) with parchment paper.

For the base, crush biscuits in a food processor until they resemble wet sand. Transfer the cookies to a bowl (if you're working with cups, you can measure them at this stage).

Pour in the melted butter. When the ingredients are combined, press the mixture into the prepared tin, and up the sides (around 2 inches). Make sure the base is coated completely to prevent any leaking. Place the tin in the fridge while you prepare the filling.

To make the filling, combine all the ingredients (cream cheese, pumpkin puree, eggs, sugar, vanilla, cinnamon, and nutmeg) and whisk until combined. The mixture will be pale yellow/orange, and may be rather thin, although the consistency will depend on the amount of water in the pumpkin as well as the cream cheese, so don't worry too much—just as long as everything is blended.

Pour the mixture into the prepared crust. Place the tin onto a baking tray lined with a piece of foil (in case of any leakage). Bake for 50–60 min or until the edges are set, but the middle will have a slight wobble—it will set as it cools. Chill the cheesecake to room temperature, then cover and chill overnight (this is key—the cheesecake is best enjoyed cold).

Before serving, pour the cream into a large bowl with the sugar and vanilla, then whip to a soft peak, using either a whisk or an electric beater. Pile the cream on the cheesecake, and top with caramel sauce and/or chopped, toasted pecans, and dust slightly with the cinnamon.

Storing: This cheesecake lasts for up to a week in the fridge if sealed and stored properly, but once you top with the cream, it should be served immediately.

Silky Chocolate Pie

Prep time: 30–40 min

Cook time: 30 min

Makes: 6–8 slices

For the base:

24 chocolate sandwich cookies (275 g / 9.7 oz / about 2 packed cups full of crumbs)

75 g / 2.6 oz (6 tablespoons) unsalted butter, melted

For the filling:

150 g / 5.3 oz (2/3 cup) granulated sugar

1/2 teaspoon salt

4 tablespoons cornstarch

2 teaspoons instant espresso powder

4 large egg yolks

750 mL / 25.4 fl oz (3 cups) whole milk

200 g / 7.1 oz dark chocolate, 62 percent cacao solids, chopped (around 1 1/3 cup)

25 g / 0.9 oz (2 tablespoons) unsalted butter

1 teaspoon vanilla extract

For the topping:

375 mL / 12.7 fl oz (1 1/2 cups) heavy whipping cream

1 1/2 tablespoons granulated sugar

2 teaspoons vanilla extract

Chocolate, to grate on top (optional)

This dark, devilish confection is not your average pie. The crust is made with crumbled chocolate cookies, which makes for a flavorful, crisp exterior. Spread atop the crust is a rich chocolate pudding, finished with a mound of whipped cream. The chocolate pudding can also be served by itself, but the pie version takes it to the next level.

Preheat the oven to 180°C or 350°F and butter a 22-cm (9-inch) springform cake tin, or a pie plate of the same diameter.

For the crust, crush the cookies, either in a food processor or by placing them in a resealable (Ziploc) bag and using a rolling pin. Empty the cookie crumbs into the springform pan and pour the melted butter over them. Stir the crumbs with the melted butter, then press the mixture into the cake tin, and about 3 cm (1 1/2 inches) up the sides.

Bake the crust for about 10 minutes or until crisp. The cookies may shrink down along the sides, which is fine. Right after baking, you can use the back of a spoon to press them up slightly and seal any cracks. Let the crust cool and turn off the oven.

To make the pudding, use a medium to large pot (don't place it on the stovetop yet!) to mix the sugar, salt, cornstarch, and instant espresso powder until incorporated. Add the egg yolks, and whisk till smooth. It should form a thick paste. Very gradually pour in the milk, 1 tablespoon at a time, stirring continuously as you do so, until all of the milk is added.

Place the saucepan over low heat and gently cook the mixture, stirring constantly, until it comes to a boil and thickens (around 10 to 15 minutes). If you lift up the spatula and run your finger along the middle, the pudding should hold its shape. Take the saucepan or pot off the heat and stir in the dark chocolate, butter, and vanilla, mixing until smooth. Pour the mixture into a glass bowl and cover with plastic wrap. Let the pudding cool, then place in the fridge for at least 2 hours.

To assemble the pie, spread the pudding into the crust, then chill the pie until you are ready to serve, around 4 hours or up to a day. Right before serving, whip the cold heavy whipping cream with the sugar and vanilla, just until it forms peaks if you lift the beaters or whisk. I like to whip it by hand, but you can do this step using an electric mixer. Dollop the mixture in the center of the pie, and sift over some cocoa powder or grated chocolate.

Unmold the pie from the tin if you used a springform cake tin. You can also serve the pie in a pie plate or dish, an easier and less stressful option that avoids breaking the crust.

Serve the pie cold, as is or with fruit.

Storing: This pie is best enjoyed within a week of making it but should be served immediately after topping with the whipped cream.

Pear Tarte Tatin

Prep time: 25–30 min

Cook time: 25–30 min

Serves: 6–8 slices

Ingredients

1 kg pears, about 7 to 8 of them if
weighted whole, with skin and core
(try to use pears that are ripe but
not mushy; pears that would be
good to eat—even slightly underripe
pears—will work fine)*

Juice of half a lemon (around
1 tablespoon)

¼ teaspoon ground cinnamon
(optional)

75 g / 2.6 oz (⅓ cup) unsalted butter

100 g / 3.5 oz (½ cup) granulated sugar

½ teaspoon salt

350 g / 12.3 oz (around 1 large
sheet) puff pastry, enough for a
22-cm/9-inch pie

To serve:

Vanilla ice cream

Flaked almonds

Confectioners' sugar or cinnamon
for dusting

If you're looking for a dessert that will literally turn your world upside down, look no further. A *tarte tatin* is essentially fruit bathed in buttery caramel sauce, covered in puff pastry that is baked until golden brown, then flipped over to reveal an impressive dessert that will be demolished as soon as you serve it. It is delicious served warm with a generous scoop of vanilla ice cream scattered with toasted almonds.

Preheat the oven to 200°C or 390°F and line a baking tray with parchment paper. Peel, quarter, and core the pears, then place in a large bowl and toss them with the lemon juice and cinnamon. Set aside.

In a saucepan or skillet (22 to 24 cm or 9 to 10 inches in diameter) over medium heat, melt the butter. Then add the sugar and salt and let the mixture come to a boil. Once the sugar begins to caramelize and turn golden, add the pears. It may seem like a lot of pears, but they will shrink as they cook. Prod the pears gently to settle them.

Once the pears are soft, turn off the heat. If your saucepan isn't ovenproof, transfer the pears to a 22-to-24-cm (9-to-10-inch) baking dish and let the mixture cool for 10 additional minutes. In the meantime, prepare the puff pastry by dusting a surface with flour and gently unrolling the dough. Cut the pastry into a large circle shape using a knife.

Place the pastry atop the pears, tucking in the excess. Prick it several times with a fork. Then place the saucepan or baking dish onto the lined baking tray and bake for 25 to 30 minutes or until the puff pastry turns a golden-brown color. Place a large plate on top and, using oven mitts or a kitchen towel, flip the *tarte* over in one swift motion. Be extremely careful: it's hot and the liquid may burn. If any pieces of pear are left behind, gently rearrange them on the *tarte*. Garnish the *tarte tatin* with flaked almonds and serve with a dusting of ground cinnamon and/or confectioners' sugar and vanilla ice cream or whipped cream. Serve warm.

Storing: The dessert can last a few days in the refrigerator and tastes delicious cold but should generally be served immediately.

Note: If you don't fancy pears, you can always replace them with apples, bananas, or peaches.

December

December has always been a highly anticipated time of year, at least in my mind, because its arrival marks the start of holiday festivities and gatherings with friends and family. Whether it's the beginning of a holiday vacation, the twinkling of fairy lights wrapped around the lampposts, or the front porches that bring warmth as the days grow darker, I cherish it all.

Since my sister and I left home for opposite ends of the world, it is in December that our family comes together to celebrate. Christmastime in Poland always includes a walk through the Old Town, hot mugs of mulled wine or hot chocolate, and enjoyment of the spectacle of lights. In the Netherlands, I've been fortunate to experience some of the *Sinterklaas* traditions with friends. On *Sinterklaas*, we give each other chocolate letters, *pepernoten*, and arrange "Secret Santas" where we write poems and exchange small gifts. Last year, I was invited to a *Gourmetten* dinner. We sat around a table for hours and grilled tiny portions of meat and veggies. I cherish these memories and look forward to making new ones each year.

To commemorate the holidays in December, I am sharing a selection of some of my favorite recipes, desserts to fit (most of) your celebratory needs. If you seek a bold dessert, the grand finale to your holiday feast, take a look at the Festive Pavlova, a lush, cloud-like meringue with a crisp exterior and marshmallow-like interior. If you're looking for treats to gift, try the Almond Toffee (a personal favorite of mine) or the Chocolate Log. And of course, no holiday is complete without cookies. The Snowball and Spiced Sugar Cookies will add to any celebration.

Festive Pavlova

Prep time: 30 min

Cook time: around 1 hour

Makes: 8–10 servings

For the meringue:

4 large egg whites

225 g / 7.9 oz (1 cup) granulated sugar

2 teaspoons cornstarch

1 teaspoon vinegar

A few drops of rose extract (optional, replace with 1 teaspoon vanilla)

A pinch of salt

For the topping:

300 mL / 10.1 fl oz (around 1¼ cup) heavy whipping cream, cold from the fridge

1 teaspoon vanilla extract

2 tablespoons granulated sugar

Fruit of your choice to decorate (I use the seeds of 1 pomegranate and 9–10 segmented mandarins, but any fruit will work nicely, such as mangoes, kiwis, berries, bananas, passionfruit pulp, etc.)

Named in honor of Russian ballerina Anna Pavlova during one of her visits to Australia and New Zealand, the precise origins of pavlova are still debated, although the dessert is a staple in both Australia and New Zealand. A billowy meringue with a crisp exterior and marshmallow-like interior, a pavlova is piled high with whipped cream and fresh fruit, making it irresistible during the summer. But why not enjoy one during the winter as well? This holiday version is bedazzled with clementine segments, pomegranate seeds, and crushed pistachios, a colorful, festive combination (but feel free to use whichever fruit you have available). People are often intimidated by the art of meringue-making, but meringues are actually not too difficult to make (just make sure to follow the tips in the recipe). And if anything goes wrong, don't worry—you can always transform this dessert into the best sort of pudding, an Eton Mess (see p. 107).

Preheat the oven to 180°C or 350°F, and line a large baking tray with greaseproof baking paper. Put the egg whites in a large, clean bowl and, using an electric mixer, beat them until they increase significantly in volume and form nice, foamy peaks when you lift up the beaters, about 3 minutes. Next, gradually add the sugar, 1 tablespoon at a time, beating constantly until the egg whites develop a glossy sheen and stiffen even more. They should somewhat resemble the appearance of melted marshmallows. This should take about 10 minutes. Beat in the cornstarch, vinegar, the rose extract, if using, and the salt.

Spoon the mixture onto the baking sheet in a 22-cm (9-inch) circle (I sometimes like to draw a circle on the back side of the baking paper with a pencil or pen so that I know approximately how big it has to be). You can swirl it into any shape; I like to create some sort of crater in the center and slightly fancier edges. I also like to leave the tray out for about 20 minutes before baking, as I find it puffs up a little more, but this is optional, the taste is the same.

Reduce the oven temperature to 150°C or 300°F, and place the meringue in the middle rack, with another empty tray on the top. Bake the meringue for 1 hour, then turn the oven off and leave the meringue there to cool for several hours before removing it. Right before serving, whip the heavy whipping cream with the vanilla and sugar until it forms soft peaks when you lift the beaters.

Spoon the cream into the cooled meringue and decorate it with fruit of your choice.

Storing: The meringue with cream and fruit should be served immediately, and the leftovers can keep for about a day in the fridge, but keep in mind that the texture or flavor will not be the same. The shell can be stored for several days if sealed properly, at room temperature without the cream and fruit.

Tip: Mastering Your Meringue

- Make sure you're using a nice, clean, big bowl. I find that a glass bowl works best for this. Any grease or dampness will prevent the egg whites from gaining volume. This also means that your eggbeaters should be completely clean and dry as well.

- Slightly stale egg whites work like magic, so if you can, crack the eggs a day in advance, refrigerate them, and then take them out about 30 mins before using.

- Use room-temperature egg whites, as they are easier to work with.

- If the egg white has any traces of yolk, it won't whip properly, so make sure that there are no strands of yellow in there!

- If you don't use an electric mixer, it will be difficult to obtain a nice, stiff peak, and it doesn't work in a blender either. You can do this by hand, but it will take a while!

- You know your egg whites are whipped enough if you hold the bowl upside down over your head and it retains its shape (it doesn't fall on your head!).

- When the meringue is baking, make sure that it is in the middle rack of the oven and that there is a tray above to prevent it from browning. Also make sure that the oven is the right temperature.

- Don't open the oven door until the baking time is done, as this might cause the meringue to crack and deflate.

Almond Toffee

Prep time: 15–20 min

Cook time: 30–40 min in total

Makes: Roughly 450 grams (1 pound) of toffee

Special equipment needed: Candy thermometer*

Ingredients

300 g / 10.6 oz (2 cups) unsalted almonds

240 g / 8.5 oz (1¼ cup) brown sugar

2 tablespoons water

100 g / 3.5 oz (½ cup) unsalted butter

¼ teaspoon baking soda

½ teaspoon vanilla extract

½ teaspoon salt (can use less)

150 g / 5.3 oz (around ¾ cup) of chocolate (semi-sweet or bittersweet both work fine, I use 100 g / 3.5 oz of dark chocolate with 70 percent cacao solids and 50 g / 1.8 oz of milk chocolate)

When I was younger, I would package this toffee in little bundles and give it to my teachers on Teacher Appreciation Day. The taste is mesmerizing, a perfect combination of sweet, salty, and crunchy, all topped with a layer of chocolate to balance the intensity of the sugar. If you prefer peanuts or hazelnuts, feel free to use those instead. A slightly more complicated aspect of this recipe is the boiling point of the toffee mixture: you'll need to have a candy thermometer handy, because estimating the temperature may not go so well (a few degrees can make a big difference when you're making candy). Give this recipe a try—it is a delicious gift and a wonderful introduction to candy-making.

Make sure to have read the recipe once, and that you have all the ingredients ready, since you'll need to work rather quickly once the toffee boils.

First, roughly chop the almonds. They should be somewhere between coarse and fine, think pea-size. Tip the almonds onto a baking tray that has been lined with a piece of parchment paper. Toast the almonds at 180°C/350°F for 8 to 10 mins or until they just start to brown and become fragrant. Let the almonds cool.

In the meantime, prepare the baking tray for the toffee. I like to make this by lining the tray with a piece of aluminum foil, and greasing the foil with a bit of butter, but you can also use a piece of parchment paper. Sprinkle half the almonds onto this tray, in a rectangular or square shape. It should be roughly 20x25 cm (8x10 inches) in size, but just use this as a guide, no need to be very precise.

Next, tip the brown sugar, water, and butter into a heavy-duty pot, and set the pot over medium heat. Stir the mixture gently, using a wooden spoon or spatula, until everything has melted, then bring the mixture to a boil. At this point, clip a candy thermometer to the side of the pan, and stop stirring the mixture. The heat should still be on medium, or medium low. When the temperature reaches 140°C or 285°F, the hard crack stage, remove it from heat. It will be extremely hot, so by all means, do not touch it.

Stir in the baking soda, vanilla, and salt, which will turn the mixture an opaque color. Next, quickly pour the hot toffee over the almonds, almost like a drizzle. You won't have time to spread it, as it hardens almost immediately, but it should spread on its own if you drizzle well. Again, be careful, it will be hot. Immediately scatter the chocolate pieces over the toffee (it won't be completely firm but don't worry) and let everything sit for 5 to 10 minutes. The heat from the toffee will melt the chocolate. Using the spatula, generously spread the chocolate over the toffee mixture. While the chocolate is still melted, sprinkle with the rest of the almonds and let everything cool completely, till the chocolate is hardened.

To speed things up, you can put it in the fridge or outside if it's cold enough!

Using a knife, cut the toffee into pieces. It should break relatively easily. You can also break the pieces with your hands.

Storing: These will last for over a week if stored in an airtight container, in the fridge. Give this one a try—it's a challenge, but so worth it.

Note: For this recipe, you really do need a candy thermometer. There are ways to get around it (i.e., dropping some of the mixture in ice-cold water), but this won't get you very accurate results and might result in the toffee being too hard or too soft. For the best toffee, invest in a thermometer—it will be worth it.

Chocolate Log

Prep time: 15 min

Cook time: 5 min

Makes: 1 log, around 30 cm (12 inches) in length

Ingredients

200 g / 7.1 oz tea biscuits (replace with graham crackers or digestive biscuits) roughly broken (2 cups of rubble)*

50 g / 1.8 oz (½ cup) walnuts (optional)

150 g / 5.3 oz (around ¾ cup) dark chocolate (at least 60 percent cacao solids)

125 mL / 4.2 fl oz (½ cup) heavy whipping cream

2 teaspoons orange zest (optional)

A pinch of salt

50 g / 1.8 oz (¼ cup) unsalted butter, cubed

This heavenly chocolate log was a treat I enjoyed often at my friend Ronnie's house, courtesy of her mom Sefi. Even as a kid, sugar was my greatest weakness: I'd return for slice after slice, a rich combination of chocolate, biscuits, and nuts. I wanted to include a recipe for a chocolate log because its intricate, artistic appearance belies its true simplicity. It is delicious and makes for a perfect gift at this time of year. I also like to infuse it with orange zest for a slight twist.

Break the cookies and the walnuts into small pieces. They should be coarse, like rubble, not sand, and will amount to 2 cups. Set the cookies aside.

Next, roughly chop the chocolate. In a medium-sized saucepan over low to medium heat, warm the heavy whipping cream along with the orange zest, if using. Bring the cream to a simmer, and when bubbles start to appear around the edges, turn the heat off. Add the chocolate to the cream, and let the mixture sit for around 30 seconds. Next, whisk the chocolate and cream together until smooth.

Toss in the salt and the butter, and stir gently until the butter has melted into the chocolate. Fold in the cookies and the walnuts, mixing till the cookies and nuts are completely coated in the chocolate.

The next step is perhaps the most challenging, as you'll need to mold the mixture into a log shape. There are several ways you can go about this. You can pour the mixture onto a generous piece of parchment paper, mush it into a log, and twist both ends to seal it, like a candy. Parchment is a good way to go about this because it's sturdy and non-stick. Just make sure the mixture is sealed in completely so that there is little to no mess. You can also use foil or plastic wrap. If this is intimidating, or if anything goes wrong, you can always press the mixture into a 20-to-24-cm (8-to-9-inch) cake tin and cut it into pieces or slices once set. Place the log in the fridge for several hours or until firm. It can take 3 hours or slightly longer, and putting it in the freezer will speed up the process slightly.

The log should be quite solid before cutting. If it's still too soft, it might crumble or not release quite as easily from the parchment. If this happens, just put it back in the fridge, as it's not done. Once it's ready, you can dust some confectioners' sugar or cocoa powder on top. You can also use a string to tie knots for a more deceptive salami-like appearance.

Slice the log into generous portions and serve.

Storing: This lasts for a week or so in the fridge.

Note I usually measure the rubble in terms of cups rather than grams because tea biscuits are a lot lighter than digestive biscuits or graham crackers.

Snowball Cookies

Prep time: 20 min

Cook time: 13–15 min

Makes: 30–40 cookies

Ingredients

225 g / 7.9 oz (1 cup) unsalted butter,
soft and room temperature

75 g / 2.6 oz (½ cup)
confectioners' sugar

1 teaspoon vanilla extract

½ teaspoon salt

325 g / 11.5 oz (2¼ cups) all-
purpose flour

125 g / 4.4 oz (1 cup) unsalted walnuts
or pecans, finely chopped

Additional confectioners' sugar
for dusting (around 150 g / 5.3
oz / 1 cup)

The first time I made these cookies was on New Year's Eve during my "gap" semester. My parents had gone to a party and I insisted on staying home because I wanted to bake cookies. And I did, three different kinds. In the end, the snowballs were deemed the winner of the evening (along with my parents, who came home right before midnight to celebrate with me). These cookies are rich, buttery, and crunchy, and pair beautifully with a fresh cup of coffee or tea. They also make for delicious gifts at this time of year. I've given several virtual cooking demonstrations to beginners on how to make this recipe, because it's foolproof and can easily be tweaked according to taste. If you like chocolate, throw in some chocolate chips. Not a fan of walnuts? Any other nut can be substituted instead. Or why not add in a bit of espresso powder for more of a coffee flair? With these cookies, the sky's the limit.

Preheat the oven to 180°C (350°F) and line a cookie tray with parchment paper. In a bowl, cream together the butter, sugar, vanilla, and salt. The mixture should be a fluffy, pale yellow mass. Next, stir in the flour. The dough should be soft, yet firm and thick.

Finally, add in the chopped nuts, mixing until everything is well-combined. I like to use a wooden spoon or spatula to do this, as the mixture is too thick for a whisk.

Roll the dough into 1-tablespoon-sized balls using your hands, and place the balls on the prepared baking tray, around 2.5 cm (1 inch) apart. Do not press the mounds of dough down, as you want them to look as much like a snowball as possible. Bake for 13 to 15 min, or until the bottoms of the cookies are just slightly golden (they will puff up slightly as they bake), then take them out of the oven and let them cool for several minutes.

In the meantime, tip the additional confectioners' sugar into a shallow dish or plate, in a mound. While the cookies are still warm, roll them in the confectioners' sugar. The coating will immediately start to melt—this is what you want. Place the cookies on a wire rack and let them cool completely. Once the cookies have cooled, roll them once more in the confectioners' sugar—this is when they really start to look like snowballs.

Serve these with tea or coffee.

Storing: These store well for 1 week in an airtight container, at room temperature or in the fridge. You can also freeze the unbaked cookie balls for several weeks.

Spiced Sugar Cookies

Prep time: 30 min

Cook time: 11–13 min

Makes: 20–30 cookies, depending on the size

For the cookies:

275 g / 9.7 oz (1¾ cups) all-purpose flour

½ teaspoon salt

½ teaspoon baking powder

1½ teaspoons ground ginger*

½ teaspoon ground cinnamon*

125 g / 4.4 oz (½ cup) unsalted butter

125 g / 4.4 oz (½ cup + 1 tablespoon) granulated sugar

1 large egg

1 teaspoon vanilla extract

For the icing:

25 g / 0.9 oz (2 tablespoons) unsalted butter, soft at room temperature

200 g / 7.1 oz (1½ cups) confectioners' sugar

1 teaspoon vanilla extract

2 tablespoons milk or water

Food coloring of choice

To me, cut-out cookies are a necessity around the holidays, and by default, so is this recipe. It's a classic all-purpose cookie recipe that falls somewhere between gingerbread and shortbread in terms of flavor. The spice is subtle, just enough to spark your tastebuds. Let your creative juices flow with these cookies; not only can you cut the dough however you like, you can also have fun decorating these. It's a wholesome activity to do with your family and friends.

To make the cookies, first combine the flour, salt, baking powder, ground ginger, and cinnamon. Whisk until incorporated, and set aside. In another bowl, cream together the butter and sugar until well-combined. Next, add in the egg and vanilla extract. Don't worry if the mixture clumps slightly; it will come together when you add the dry ingredients.

Gradually add in the flour mixture and switch to a rubber spatula if necessary. The mixture will be thick and may be a little sticky. Scoop the cookie dough onto a piece of plastic wrap, covering it well. Shape the dough into a small disk. This ensures that a skin does not form on the dough, and it remains smooth.

Chill the dough for at least two hours or overnight, or until it is firm to the touch. The longer the dough chills, the more pronounced the spice flavors will be. When you're ready to bake the cookies, preheat the oven to 180°C or 350°F and line a baking tray with parchment paper. If the dough has been chilling for several hours, leave it for around 10 minutes to soften slightly, as it will be quite firm.

Dust a work surface and the dough with flour and roll to a ½-cm or ¼-inch thickness. Using cookie cutters, cut the dough as you like. Fear not if you don't have cookie cutters: you can do several things. You could roll the dough into a log instead of a disk when refrigerating, then slice the log into ½-cm or ¼-inch slices. You could also roll the dough into 1-tablespoon-sized balls, roll the balls in granulated sugar, then put them on the cookie sheet and press down to form a disk. Alternatively, you can use the rim of a glass to cut out shapes. Gather the scraps, then roll out the cookie dough again, adding a touch more flour when necessary to prevent sticking.

Place the cut-outs onto the parchment-lined baking tray and bake the cookies for 11 to 13 minutes, or until the edges are a light golden brown (11 minutes will give you a slightly softer cookie, 13 minutes will give you a slightly crunchier cookie). Let the cookies cool for several minutes on the tray, then transfer them to a wire rack and let them cool completely before icing.

To make the icing, use a wooden spoon to combine the butter and confectioners' sugar as best you can. It will be relatively dry. At this stage, add the vanilla, followed by the milk or water a little at a time, until you obtain your desired consistency. If the icing ends up being too thin, add some more sugar. If it's too thick, add more milk. If you'd like, you can color the icing with your food coloring of choice.

Spread the icing onto the cookies, using a butter knife or using a piping bag with the end snipped off just slightly, and top with sprinkles. Wait until the icing has hardened (this takes around an hour, or less if refrigerated) before stacking or serving. The icing makes enough for the cookies specified in the recipe, but if you'd like to have multiple colors, you might like to double the icing recipe so that there is enough per color.

Storing: These cookies last for around a week once frosted, and slightly longer unfrosted. The dough, unbaked, freezes well too!

Notes:

- These do spread slightly, but not too much—so they're really nice for rolling. The recipe can very easily be doubled to make more.

- You can omit the spices if you prefer a vanilla sugar cookie instead.

Bittersweet Endings

With December coming to a close, it is time to look back and reflect on all the memories the past year has brought. It is a bittersweet moment, saying goodbye to another year, but welcoming a new one. In closing, I would like to thank you for letting me share a year of sweets with you. It has been a pleasure putting this book together, from selecting the recipes, to photographing them, to writing them, and now presenting them to you. I hope you have enjoyed 52 Weeks, *52 Sweets*, and that this book is something that you can refer to all year-round and for many years to come.

Acknowledgments

I would first and foremost like to thank my viewers and readers, and my family and my friends, for their overwhelming support. I am eternally grateful for all their encouragement.

There are a few people in particular that I would like to express my gratitude toward, without whom this book would not have been possible. To Radhika and Aditya, thank you for your advice and help right at the beginning, and Maya, thank you for your help at the end. To my housemates over the years, thank you for bearing with all the trails of sugar and chocolate I left behind, and for sharing your own passions for food with me. To Lourdes, thank you for painting beautiful backdrops that I could use in my photography, and for all your help in my dire hours of need, to Minilliah, thank you for your support and style inspiration: I owe many beautiful photos to you! To my photography guru Kinga, thank you for sharing your wisdom, and for nurturing my love of photography. To my grandparents, Dadaji, Dadiji, Dapapa, and Ashama, thank you for your constant encouragement and kind words. To Sefi, Ronnie, Danika, and her father, Noah, and his family, Ms. Sutton, Ms. Hay, and Mrs. Matter, thank you for sharing your delicious recipes and inspirations. To my FocusCo board members, my ASW friends, my UCU friends and teachers, my LRM classmates, our neighbors, Samarth, the Bhandaris and Yadavs, thank you for your support and encouragement. To Tama, thank you for helping with the numerical stuff, keeping up with my incessant food babble, for being a grounding force in particularly stressful times.

This book would not have been possible without Neha, Dad, and Mom. Neha, thank you for acting as my occasional hand model, for your brutal (but necessary) honesty, for always pushing me to reach my potential, and for being a constant source of inspiration. Dad, thank you for instilling in me a love of food, for working so hard every day so that our options are never limited, and for letting me fill your grocery basket with mounds of sugar. Thank you, Mom, for filming my very first video, when it all began, for helping me grow in every way possible, for the endless grocery store trips, for cleaning dish after dish after dish, for helping me paint backdrops, for driving me across town to buy plates I could use as food props—you are my rock, I don't know how I would have done this without you.

Thank you to the entire Mango team for putting together a beautiful book. And finally, thank you to my editor Jane, for choosing me, for believing in me, and for guiding me along the way. I am eternally grateful to you for making my dream come true.

About the Author

Vedika Luthra was born in India, raised in Poland (where she attended an American school), and then moved to the Netherlands where she is currently pursuing postgraduate studies. Her unique background has shaped her experiences in the kitchen. Passionate about food from an early age, Vedika started her food blog *Hot Chocolate Hits* when she was fourteen. Her first videos were her favorite recipes, such as classic brownies, lemon cake, and coconut cake. A year after she began posting videos, she was recruited by food video network Tastemade as one of their network partners on YouTube. With their help and her dedication, *Hot Chocolate Hits* amassed a following, hungry for recipes such as mango cheesecake and chocolate chip cookie lava cakes. In 2015, her recipe for no-bake Oreo bars was one of the first videos on their "Sweeten" page to go viral, amassing 36 million views in the first year. She has since combined her passion for photography, video, and baking into an inviting and popular channel, *Hot Chocolate Hits*. In addition to her passion for food and photography, Vedika also enjoys writing and has written about food for several publications including *Food52, Spoon University*, and more.

Index

Notes

Notes

Mango Publishing, established in 2014, publishes an eclectic list of books by diverse authors—both new and established voices—on topics ranging from business, personal growth, women's empowerment, LGBTQ studies, health, and spirituality to history, popular culture, time management, decluttering, lifestyle, mental wellness, aging, and sustainable living. We were recently named 2019 *and* 2020's #1 fastest-growing independent publisher by *Publishers Weekly*. Our success is driven by our main goal, which is to publish high-quality books that will entertain readers as well as make a positive difference in their lives.

Our readers are our most important resource; we value your input, suggestions, and ideas. We'd love to hear from you—after all, we are publishing books for you!

Please stay in touch with us and follow us at:
Facebook: Mango Publishing
Twitter: @MangoPublishing
Instagram: @MangoPublishing
LinkedIn: Mango Publishing
Pinterest: Mango Publishing
Newsletter: mangopublishinggroup.com/newsletter

Join us on Mango's journey to reinvent publishing, one book at a time.